APPROACHING
MORMONS
LOVE
IN

WILBUR LINGLE

APPROACHING MORMONS L⟨IN⟩VE

How to Witness Effectively
Without Arguing

WILBUR LINGLE

CLC ✦ PUBLICATIONS
Fort Washington, Pennsylvania 19034

Published by CLC ❖ Publications

U.S.A.
P.O. Box 1449, Fort Washington, PA 19034

GREAT BRITAIN
51 The Dean, Alresford, Hants. SO24 9BJ

AUSTRALIA
P.O. Box 419M, Manunda, QLD 4879

NEW ZEALAND
10 MacArthur Street, Feilding

ISBN 0-87508-777-9

Copyright © 2005
Wilbur Lingle

Contents

Chapter One

Introduction

IN 1975 (when I was a Christian missionary in Japan, where I served from 1954 to 1989) I probably knew as much about Mormonism as the average American. I knew that Joseph Smith was the founder. I had heard the story about the gold plates that *The Book of Mormon* supposedly was translated from. I recognized the name of Brigham Young as having been one of the early Latter-day Saints leaders. I also knew that many Mormons lived in Utah and that Salt Lake City was their headquarters. However, in March of 1975 when two American Mormon "elders" (ie., missionaries) approached me and wanted me to study Mormonism with them, it started me on the road of investigating Mormonism in depth, and this has resulted in my witnessing to many Mormons since that time.

Frustrated! This describes my condition when I started witnessing to those Mormon missionaries. As we talked together I realized that we were using many of the same terms—but had entirely different meanings for them. In order to try and find help in my witnessing, I read every book about the sect I could get my hands on. But while these books gave me "facts" about Mormonism, they did not give me the needed approach in order to be a successful witness to its adherents.

Only after exhaustively studying Mormonism by reading Mormon-published books and conversing with many Mormons did I, through the process of "trial and error," come up with a successful means of witnessing to those who belong to the Church of Jesus Christ of Latter-day Saints (LDS for short). I also became aware that there are many Christians who would like to be effective witnesses to Mormons, but most do not know how; nor do they have the time to study LDS doctrine and teachings in depth. Because I did not find the necessary material in print to help me in my witnessing, I now want to share the results of my study and my subsequent witnessing with as many people as possible.

As I dealt with more and more Mormons, I found that they were usually very bold and forward at first; but as I took time to fellowship with individuals among them, over a period of time I discovered just how empty they were in their hearts—and I longed to be able to share the wonderful message of our Lord and Savior Jesus Christ effectively with each one. The average Mormon does not have the faintest idea what Biblical Christianity is all about or how he can come into a personal relationship with the Lord Jesus Christ. In fact, Mormons are *forbidden* to have an intimate relationship with Jesus Christ! If we as born-again Christians do not take the time and make the effort to win their confidence so that we can present the way of salvation to them clearly, it negates the possibility of their trusting the Savior. Remember, in most cases it is *we* who are approached by the Mormons, so should we not take advantage of these opportunities and learn *how* we can witness successfully to them? *When you see a Mormon come to know Christ as his personal Savior,* it will be worth all the time, effort, prayer and love you put into it!

The Church of Jesus Christ of Latter-day Saints, better known as Mormonism, is one of the fastest-growing religious groups today. In almost every city or town of any size, you will see one of their meeting places. Utah used to be known as "Mormon country," but now there are more Mormons outside of Utah than in it. They have over 60,000 missionaries in America and around the world! (This compares to 42,000 evangelical missionaries sent out from the United States by all the different Protestant mission groups and denominations combined.)

Not too many years ago the average Christian had never met a Mormon, but today that has changed. Many families have been affected directly, because someone they know has been converted to Mormonism. Pastors have seen people to whom they have been ministering swept into the Mormon Church. Many Christian homes have been visited by Mormon missionaries, with much confusion as a result.

But you might ask, "What can I do about the situation? Though I am a born-again Christian, I am only one person. I need help!" You will not find an easy avenue, or one with slick shortcuts, presented in this book. However, I will set forth an *effective* way for you to give a positive testimony for Christ whenever you come in contact with a member of the LDS Church— a way whereby you could lead him to Christ.

But first, let me set the stage. If you are Mr. or Mrs. Average Christian, you may be asking: "When these nice-looking, well-dressed strangers knock at my door and want to talk with me about religion, should I invite them in? Shouldn't I just say, 'No, thank you, I'm not interested'? Mr. Lingle, I understand that Mormonism is a *cult*—a false religion. Doesn't the Bible forbid me to speak to them? That's what some of my friends have told me."

A Fundamental Point

The Relation of 2 John 10–11 to Witnessing to Cultists

Whenever the subject of witnessing to a cultist—a Jehovah's Witness, a Mormon, or such—is raised, a short passage of Scripture (if you are a Bible-loving Christian) may come to mind, namely 2 John 10–11. These verses state: "If there come any unto you, and bring not this doctrine, receive him not into your house, neither bid him Godspeed: for he that biddeth him Godspeed is partaker of his evil deeds." Many Christians, therefore, will have nothing to do with anyone involved in a cult, because of these two prohibitive verses. For many years I prided myself on being able to tell these proselytizers that I believed them to be members of a false cult; I would not let them into my house or waste my time talking to them. However, as I began to get involved in witnessing to lost sinners, I was forced to wonder whether my approach was correct. The reasons for this are three-fold:

1. Cultists are taught that all Christians are rude. A Christian proves that this teaching is true when he says that the Mormon is a member of a false cult and then slams the door in his face. This approach only plays into the hands of the cultist, and encourages him in his religion.

2. I realized that I was taking 2 John 10–11 out of context and was not harmonizing it with the rest of Scripture. For example, Romans 12:20 says, "Therefore, if thine enemy hunger, feed him; if he thirst, give him drink: for in so doing thou shalt heap coals of fire on his head." In John 3, Nicodemus the Pharisee came to see Jesus and was welcomed by Him. Some of the strongest words Jesus ever used were against the sect of the Pharisees—they certainly did not have the same doctrine as Jesus. However, we know that Nicodemus became a true disciple of Jesus because Jesus welcomed him and explained the plan of salvation to him.

3. I realized that I was missing a great opportunity. I had traveled thousands of miles to reach the Japanese people for the Savior. Many faithful Christians were giving and praying so that I could be a witness there. It is a long, slow process in Japan to make a contact and develop a relationship with an individual so

one can witness to him or her. And here I was, turning away English-speaking young men who came right to my door asking for an opportunity to talk. I would willingly invite a Buddhist Japanese into my house to witness to him, but I was refusing to witness to a Mormon or a Jehovah's Witness!

I began to do some serious thinking about the subject of witnessing to cultists. I did not want to be disobedient to the Bible, but I did want to witness to those in the cults. Was there a solution to this problem? Was there more to the meaning of 2 John 10–11 than what I had always been taught? I spent much time in prayer and study and was led to what I feel is the true application of these verses—and then was surprised to find out that many others had come to the same conclusion.

When one wants to find out the true meaning of Scripture, it is usually helpful to learn about the setting in which the verses were written.

The Bible clearly urges Christians to offer hospitality to other Christians. Paul often refers to the hospitality that he received from fellow believers as he journeyed from place to place. At the time that the New Testament books were written, most hotels and inns were houses of ill-repute. (Even today, many hotels and inns are like this.) Traveling Christians did not want to stay in these places of sin and temptation, so they had to find lodging somewhere else. For this reason, Christians would commonly open up their homes and offer hospitality to traveling Christians. In fact, in the ruins of an ancient Roman town archaeologists have found the sign of a fish (much like that seen on bumper stickers today) in the walkway at the entrance to a house. This fish sign indicated that a Christian lived there who would provide lodging for Christian travelers. This symbol made it easier for a traveling believer to find a congenial place to stay.

Also in that century, most of the churches met in private homes. Church leaders needed to be careful not to welcome heretics or cultists into these house churches and recognize them as true Christians, giving them an opportunity to speak to the congregation.

It was in *this* light that 2 John 10–11 was written. Christians were to welcome other Christians into their homes for food and lodging, but they were not to do the same for those in the cults who would seek to destroy the gospel. They were not to offer them free lodging or permit them to proclaim their false teachings at their church meetings. I believe this is the type of hospitality that is forbidden by 2 John 10–11. It was not meant to keep Christians from witnessing to cultists in their homes.

So when the advocate of some other religious view comes to my door, wishing to discuss the Bible or his own sacred scripture with me, should I turn him away? If I am not willing to lovingly reason with him, to enlighten him to the facts of the gospel of salvation, how is he to come to a knowledge of the truth? As a disciple of Christ, am I not obligated to seize every God-given opportunity to witness for my Lord? And here at my door is a potential candidate for heaven! "Lord, what do You want me to do?"

Accepting the Challenge

Admittedly, witnessing to a cultist is not quite the same as opening your Bible and explaining the simple gospel to a child in your Sunday School class; or praying with a repentant seeker at the City Mission; or even discussing Christian doctrine with a friendly neighbor. Quite obviously, your approach must be different than in those situations.*

The courteous callers at your door (usually there are *two* young men) would like to make an appointment to discuss their faith—

---

* But perhaps you have a good neighbor—or maybe a relative—who is a Mormon, and your heart's desire is to effectively witness to him. Can this book be of value to you? Yes. See the postscript at the end of this chapter.

and yours. They would prefer having a *series* of meetings with you. Fine! As God's spirit leads you, schedule an agreeable time for them to come back—preferably once a week—to discuss "religion." They will be happy to oblige.

Mormon missionaries would like to meet with you at least seven times, as their lesson plans (mostly in video presentations) are set up for this number of visits. Good! However, you don't want to seem to give in to their request too easily. So, when they persist in their sales talk, say, "I feel that religion is very important. It would be difficult to decide about a religion in just one conversation. Are you able to come back for a number of times, say ten times?" It is important to get a *firm commitment* from them at the very beginning, because it will be difficult to get one later. (However, if the circumstances are such that you can have only one conversation with them, grasp even that opportunity to witness to them—because the Lord can bless any good seed that is sown.) They are usually glad to come back—until you begin to question their beliefs. At that point, they will leave and not show up again if you don't already have a *firm commitment* from them.

If they choose to honor their commitment, they will usually run out of new things to say by the fourth or fifth visit. You will then have an opportunity to present the plan of salvation more adequately. But at every meeting you want to make them *think* and *question* their beliefs. They may be defensive or argumentative at first, but if they realize that you are sincere, they will listen to what you have to say. After the fifth visit they usually get much more friendly, which enables you to make your witness more effective; but the first five are necessary to get to this point.

One incident I remember well. I had two missionaries promise me they would come back ten times. After five times, they knew they were not making progress, but since they had promised "ten times" they said they would keep their promise. The last five times we had wonderful conversations about the true gospel as found in Jesus Christ, and they listened well.

Here are two very important things you must remember when witnessing to a Mormon—or, for that matter, to any cultist.

1. You must first build a meaningful relationship of trust. This is done by spending time asking about personal things and remembering what the individual has said. I always try to recall something personal that my visitor mentioned the week before. In this way you show your friend that you have listened to him and are interested in him as a person. When you listen well to what a person is saying, you give him dignity by your listening. You cannot *witness* well unless you can *listen* well. (This is a skill I had to pick up when I first started witnessing.) *Show* them what a Christian is before you *tell* them. Your actions are very important! You will need a lot of patience and endurance. At first their minds will probably be closed to your statements, but they can read your actions loud and clear.

When meeting for discussion, you ought never to exceed one hour at a time, and you should spend half of this time building a meaningful relationship. It is not a waste of time, but *absolutely necessary*. After you have built up a friendly relationship your witnessing will be much more effective.

2. Mormons have been taught not to think for themselves nor ever to question the leaders of the LDS Church. Hence it is very difficult for them to think clearly on their own. Therefore you must patiently teach them how to think by asking thought-provoking questions on material they are not familiar with and do not have a pat answer for. It is a sad fact that most of the arguments presented to Mormons by Christians are standardized, and the Mormon missionaries have a ready response *memorized* for them. (I have two eye-opening books in my library written by Mormons. One is titled: *One Minute Answers to Anti-Mormon Questions*. The other is: *Answering Challenging Mormon Questions. Replies to 130 Queries by Friends and Critics of the LDS Church.*)

The fact that the Mormon missionaries could not think logically when it came to religious matters was something hard for me to grasp when I first started witnessing to them. Nor did they ever want to seriously consider any problems in their religion. As long as a cultist feels that he is right, his mind will be closed to any presentation of the gospel; thus, early on you need to ask *thought-provoking* questions concerning what he believes. Your aim is to get him to *think*. You should not be overly interested in the answers you receive—some of them will be "off the wall"— because your intent is to plant a seed of doubt. (How to do this is the thrust of this book.)

Most Mormons do not know their own religion in depth. They have been well trained in their basic beliefs and have been taught how to attack the beliefs of other religious groups. They know that if they can get a person to question what he believes, he will be more open to Mormonism. (I have reversed the process.) This makes it necessary to be well prepared when you witness to them. The Mormon missionaries are told to ask questions in such a way that they will get the answer they seek. If they do not get the desired response the first time, they ask further questions until they receive the answer they want. The questions the Mormons routinely use are found in a booklet that gives them instructions on how to proselytize a person. For this reason, it is best to approach them from an angle they are *not prepared for*. In short, you need to know how to question *them!*

Some of the questions they will pose are actually trick questions. For example, they may ask you, "If a person was intending to restore the church, isn't it logical that he would need the proper authority?" If you answer "Yes," you are buying into the story that Joseph Smith was given divine authority to reform the straying church. If instead you say "No," they will respond, "Do you mean that anyone can go out and restore the church without having authority?" Either answer gets you into a trap. The true church of

Jesus Christ was never lost, however, so there has never been any need for anyone to *restore* it; thus the question is not a valid one.

Also, Mormons will try to sell you on the idea that the Bible needs to be officially interpreted and so there is a need for modern-day revelations; and hence modern-day prophets are necessary to interpret the Bible and to receive and dispense modern-day revelations. They ignore the fact that the Holy Spirit was sent to properly interpret the Bible (John 14:26) and so we Christians have all that we need for life and godliness in the Bible itself (2 Peter 1:3). We do not need any modern-day revelations.

When witnessing to religionists of any stripe, your object is to present the plan of salvation in a way that can be easily understood. You should not be trying to win an argument. If you make an outright attack on anyone's beliefs, you will put them on the defensive and they will have no disposition to listen to what you have to say. Some important DO NOTs for effectively reaching Mormons are:

1. Do not attack the doctrine of polygamy.

2. Do not call Joseph Smith a false prophet, or attack *The Book of Mormon* and the gold plates at the beginning of your conversation. (I will show you later on how you *can* use Smith's questionable tale to your advantage in witnessing.)

3. Do not quote Revelation 22:18–19. These verses say that nothing is to be added to or subtracted from the Bible. The Mormon will respond with Deuteronomy 4:2 which says, "Ye shall not add unto the word which I command you, neither shall ye diminish ought from it, that ye may keep the commandments of the Lord your God which I command you." They will ask you if this verse means that nothing was to be added to the Bible after Moses wrote this section. Obviously, most of the books of the Bible were written *after* Deuteronomy.

4. Do not be rude to any Mormon; do not call him a member of a false cult or declare that he is of the devil and on his way

to hell. (According to the LDS Church only murderers and apostate Mormons go to hell, which they call "the second death.") He has been taught that all Christians are arrogant and rude. You will only hurt your testimony if you live up to his expectations.

5. Do not start by quoting Bible verses. Most of the Scripture passages cited by Christians when talking with a cultist are standardized. So the well-trained missionary has been taught these passages along with a very good argument against them. More than likely, he will tie you in a knot. Remember, to the Mormons, Scripture is *not* the final authority. Their final authority is the teachings of their leaders.

6. Do not argue. Try your utmost to avoid getting in an argument. When two people are arguing, the person not speaking at the moment is busy formulating his reply rather than giving undivided attention to the other. But your aim is to get the full attention of the person you want to reach. You can best do this by showing him some of the difficulties embedded in his beliefs—via questions. As he tries to defend his beliefs, he will often get confused. Once that happens, you can use the Scriptures in a spiritually effective way. You have to prepare his heart to "hear" the Word of God.

Concluding Counsel

To reiterate, the Mormon's system of proselytizing is what I call "a one-way street." As long as you sit and listen to everything the missionaries (college-age kids, usually—though they call each other "elder")* say, avoid asking questions that will make them think and seemingly agree with their propaganda, they will be happy to come back. However, they do not appreciate intelligent confrontation or like serious questions about their beliefs. You will discover that they cannot stand up under pressure. And they

---

* Single women, who are called "sisters," and mature couples may also serve as missionaries.

have been cleverly trained to get out of any situation that they feel they cannot handle. If you put too much pressure on them, they will protest: "I sense that you have a contentious spirit. I will not argue with you, so I must leave." What they are really saying is, "It's getting too hot for me to handle, so I have to find a way to get clear." You need to anticipate this before you begin talking to them.

Cultists are driven to believe that everything they are practicing is right. A Mormon is not supposed to question any LDS doctrine he is taught. If he does question it in his heart, he feels guilty. It is rare for any of them to accept Christ after only one conversation. So—let me stress this point again—to witness most effectively, you must get the elders to agree to come back a number of times. This needs to be done *before* any other conversation takes place.

Postscript

Perhaps the Mormons whom you know are not young missionaries from another state but are individuals living in your community—a next-door neighbor, a family down the block, a co-worker, or maybe a mature couple whom you met recently at your social club. And the Lord has shown you their spiritual need and burdened your heart for them. Or it could be that you have a Mormon relative for whom you have long been praying. Or he may be a *recent* convert to Mormonism! If any of these is the case, then *you* are the one who needs to take the initiative—but how?

The first step is to build some kind of relationship. It is best not to try to witness to a person until you have gotten acquainted. Talk to your neighbor over the back fence. Be more than perfunctory in greeting your fellow worker. Give your friend or relative a call once in a while. In many cases it will be the *Mormon* who will bring up the religious issue, and then you can proceed as I have suggested in this book.

Or, after you get to know your neighbor you might say, "I notice that the whole family is dressed up and leaves the house together on Sunday mornings. What is the special occasion?" This will usually open a door to beginning a conversation about the Mormon religion.

In the workplace, Mormons are often rather outspoken about their beliefs. I don't think it is ethical to witness to a fellow worker on company time. (At lunch time, or at a break, it is okay.) So you might consider inviting him over for an evening to get acquainted. Be sure to go slow, however, and keep working on building a relationship.

How to reach a relative? You might approach him, after you find out he is a Mormon, by saying, "You are my relative. I don't know a lot about the Mormons; I wonder if sometime we might get together to discuss the matter?" In most cases, people will be more than glad to.

Of course, don't ever attack anyone's beliefs right away, but listen to him and question him as to what he has said. This book provides many questions that are designed to make any Mormon think!

•   •   •

To witness effectively to a Mormon you need first to have a basic understanding of LDS history, doctrines, and definitions. The following three chapters are devoted to these subjects. I have also inserted three brief chapters to help you grasp a few more characteristics of the LDS religious system. Then, in chapters 8–14, we return to the topic of practical evangelism with Mormons: how to witness effectively and avoid arguments.

Chapter Two

A Brief History of
Joseph Smith and Mormonism

JOSEPH SMITH was born in the town of Sharon, Vermont, on December 23, 1805. When he was 10 years old, the family moved to Palmyra, in Wayne County, upstate New York. Four years later they moved a few miles south to the village of Manchester. There were nine children in the Smith family. Joseph did not have much formal education but appears to have been an avid reader. He had a good imagination. In 1822, he hired himself out to help dig a well for Willard Chase. At this time a colorful egg-shaped rock was found, and Joseph asked to borrow it. He claimed that he could discover things by putting the stone in his hat and looking into it. This stone later became known as the "peep stone" or the "seer stone." With this stone Joseph Smith began his work of money-digging. He claimed that by using the stone he could see buried treasure, and people began to hire him to help them hunt for such treasures. In 1826, he was arrested on charges of fraud and was found guilty. Court records have been found of the trial. Even though he was found guilty, he was not fined but was given "leg-bail." That meant that, since he was young, he was to get out of the area and not come back. If he did come back, he would be sentenced. So he did not return openly.

Joseph had been asked by Josiah Stoal to come to South Bainbridge, Chenango County, New York, to help hunt for a treasure cache. While there he boarded with Mr. Isaac Hale of Harmony, Susquehanna County, Pennsylvania. As a result of his money-digging in that area, he was brought to trial.

While staying with the Hales, Joseph met their daughter Emma. Mr. Hale did not like Joseph because Joseph did not have permanent work but spent his time in money-digging. Hale would not give Joseph permission to marry his daughter, so on January 18, 1827, Emma Hale and Joseph Smith were married secretly. They went to Manchester to live with Joseph's parents. Eight months later he returned to Harmony to take possession of some furniture and livestock that Emma owned under her name. Mr. Hale was enraged and said to Joseph, "You have stolen my daughter and married her; I had much rather have followed her to her grave. You spend your time in digging for money—pretending to see in a stone, thus aiming to deceive people." Joseph, it is reported, promised at this time to give up his "glad-looking."

Not surprisingly, Joseph found it difficult to settle down to labor on a farm. It was during this period that Joseph Smith later claimed to have found some golden plates with the help of the stone, and then began working on *The Book of Mormon*. It was published early in 1830. His original intent in writing the book was to make money. He was able to persuade a rich farmer, Martin Harris, to finance the book for him.

At this same time, Joseph Smith turned to religion. He had never been notably righteous or religious before. He says of his early days: "I frequently fell into many foolish errors and displayed the weakness of youth and the corruption of human nature, which I am sorry to say, led me into divers temptations, to the gratification of my appetites offensive in the sight of God"

(*Times and Seasons*, Vol. 3, p. 749). During this period, Smith claimed to have had many visions and revelations.

The church was officially organized on April 6, 1830, at the home of Mr. Peter Whitmer, Sr., in Fayette, New York. In the same year, Smith was brought to trial in Colesville for religious fraud. The trial lasted 23 hours and the prosecutor called 43 witnesses. The evidence was sufficient to convince Judge Knoble that Smith was a "vagrant idler," a "liar," a "deceiver," and "anything but a good man." However, there was nothing that he could be legally convicted of in his new role of prophet, seer, and revelator. Judge Knoble, having respect for the letter of the law, was obliged to dismiss the charges.

Sidney Rigdon, who had once been a Baptist pastor but had converted to the Church of Christ, had a colony of believers in Kirtland, Ohio, near Cleveland. He apparently did not get along very well with his new-found group. Rigdon heard about *The Book of Mormon* and Joseph Smith, and invited Smith and his group to come to Kirtland in 1831. Joseph Smith tried to set up a communal society in Kirtland. The people would be allowed to use the land which the church owned but the profits would go to the church. The constituents would keep whatever money was necessary for their livelihood, with the rest of the money going to the church—which was to share it with those in need. Smith set up "The United Order," supposedly as the result of a revelation from God. By 1837, however, the communal society had nearly collapsed. Smith also started his own bank, but it too failed. So he borrowed money (most of which he could not repay) to try to continue the work there.

Some Mormons (as they were now being called) who had gone to Missouri ran into a lot of opposition from the "Gentiles" (their name for non-Mormons). Because the Mormons were teaching that they were the true church and that everyone else was wrong, there was friction in the neighborhood. Neither the

Gentiles nor the Mormons were completely justified in their actions, but the Mormons were ultimately driven out of the area. Joseph Smith tried to remedy the situation, but eventually found himself in a Missouri jail. He had hoped to make Independence, Missouri, the center of his religious movement, but the Mormons were expelled from there, so Smith turned back eastward to Illinois. There, on the Mississippi River, he established a settlement which was meant to be a new Zion. He named it Nauvoo.

The Mormons founded Nauvoo in 1839 and it soon became a large town. This time Smith modified his communal plan. He set up a land company, which bought all the land and then sold it to the people. He tried to initiate industrial development along with farming. Back in Kirtland, a temple had been built. Another temple was now started in Nauvoo. Smith was not only the head of the church, he was also the mayor of the town and a commander of the Legion (militia). For a short period of time it looked as if the Mormons had found the peace they sought. But once again, because of their attitude of superiority and the power they manifested when they voted as a block, there was trouble. Furthermore, polygamy (engaged in clandestinely before) became more openly practiced. Friction between the Mormons and Gentiles grew.

A group of Mormons became discontented with some of the practices of Joseph Smith. Many of them were against polygamy, and one, William Law, openly opposed Smith. He published his own newspaper, the *Nauvoo Expositor*, to give expression to his views. Smith realized that he had a problem on his hands. As mayor of the town, he called a town council and issued a proclamation declaring the *Expositor* to be a public nuisance. A portion of the Legion marched to the *Expositor*'s office, wrecked the press, jumbled the type, and burned every issue of the hated paper that could be found. Mayor Joseph Smith was responsible, so charges of riot and treason were brought against him and his brother Hyrum. Smith assumed that if they were tried in Nauvoo they would probably be found innocent. However, they were ordered to stand trial in Carthage, a nearby town. First they refused to go. Then they tried to escape to Missouri. But, in due course, after being accused of cowardice, they returned and went to Carthage. On the evening of June 27, 1844, while the two men were imprisoned at the Carthage jail, it was attacked by a mob and they both were killed. It should be noted that they did not die as martyrs, however, for Joseph had in hand a smuggled-in six-shooter and there was a regular shoot-out, two of the attackers being mortally wounded.

After the death of Joseph Smith, Brigham Young assumed leadership of the Mormon church. The Mormons continued to have trouble in Illinois, and on February 4, 1846, the first party of the "Saints" departed from Nauvoo and crossed the Mississippi River on a journey to the West—their original destination being Oregon or Vancouver Island. This first group arrived in Salt Lake Valley on October 16, 1847. Brigham Young was a good organizer; he laid out Salt Lake City, and from there Mormon pioneers began to branch out to other parts of Utah. For a while, Brigham Young was both governor of the territory and president of the Mormon church. Under his leadership, polygamy began to spread rapidly,* as well as other practices and doctrines such as the teaching that Adam was actually God. That tenet is now the source of much embarrassment to the Mormon church, and is denied by them today even though, as the second president of the Mormon church, Young was supposedly a true prophet of God and his words were to be taken as Scripture.

From its beginning, the Mormon church has been a missionary church. Even in the early days, their missionaries were sent to England and other parts of Europe. At that time, many Europe-

---

* The Mormon church's advocacy of polygamy was for a long time a bar to the admission of Utah to the Union, but the enforcement of the Edmunds Act in 1882 led to a formal abandonment of polygamy as a tenet by the Mormons in 1890, and Utah was admitted to statehood in 1896.

ans were considering immigration to America. Mormon missionaries made great promises to them. They arranged for shiploads
of people to cross the Atlantic, even helping to pay their fare.
These newcomers traveled by steamboat up the Mississippi to
Illinois. Brigham Young had designed two-wheel pushcarts which
many immigrants then pushed across Iowa, Nebraska and Wyo-
ming to Utah.* Some of the new settlers found that Utah was
not as wonderful as they had expected and considered leaving.
However, they were indebted to the Mormon church because it
had helped to pay for their transportation, and so were unable to
move elsewhere though they wanted to.

For many years, the Mormons in Utah were encouraged to
remain there. Others were urged to come to Utah so they would
not have to associate with Gentiles. Mormon authorities controlled most of the state and all of the economy. It was difficult to
find a good job without the aegis of the Mormon church. In
recent years, however, Mormons have been encouraged to move
to other places to help in the expansion of the church. Since
1960, their worldwide membership has grown from 1.6 million
to more than 11 million. Some of the growth is due to the fact

---

* Brigham Young led the first ox-drawn wagon-train migration of 1600 Mormons from Nauvoo—Smith's failed Utopia—across the Great Plains and
through passes of the Rocky Mountains to "Zion" in 1846–47. This established the route of the Mormon Trail. The mass migration of the "Saints" was
in 1848. Use of the trail by migrants continued on and off until the completion of the Pacific Railroad in 1869.

Astoundingly, between 1856 and 1860, the handcart companies composed
of 1,962 immigrants pushed or pulled 655 handcarts as they walked 1,300
miles to the Promised Land.

Mormonism's early history includes episodes that read like a spellbinding
novel—peopled, as it is, with larger-than-life characters who perform many
outstanding feats. The "Saints'" successful westward trek against impossible
odds will surely stir any reader's imagination. But viewed from the perspec-
tive of Truth, the tale as a whole—because it is built on a monstrous mass of
deceit—must be judged an American tragedy.

How fascinating! and yet how sad!

that they have large families, and because their children are accepted into the church at eight years of age. However, their missionary program is also extremely effective, and growth has been tremendous. In 1950, there were 7,000 missionaries; now there are 60,000. If each missionary won only four converts a year, that would mean 240,000 new Mormons in that time. Their overseas missionary program, which operates in more than 40 countries, is very aggressive also. In Japan alone there are 1,900 LSD missionaries, which equals the total of Protestant evangelical missionaries in Japan. Approximately one-third of all male Mormons at the age of 19 give two years of their lives to the church at their own expense.

The Mormon church is working to reach its goal for multiplying members and missionaries. Bible-believing Christians need to be aware of the danger of the Mormon church so that they will not be deceived. (Yes, I have heard of a number of born-again Christians who have joined the Mormon church.)

Why have so many people over the years become "Latter-day Saints," especially in the early days? Because the Mormon church makes promises that will attract selfish people.

> Great promises are made to such as embrace it, signs and wonders are to attend them, such as healing the sick, the blind made to see, the lame to walk, etc; and they are to receive an everlasting inheritance in "the land of Missouri," where the Saviour will make his second appearance; at which place the foundation of the temple of God, and the City of Zion, have recently been laid, and are soon to be built. It is also to be a city of Refuge, and a safe asylum where the storms of vengeance shall pour upon the earth, and those who reject *The Book of Mormon* shall be swept off as with a besom [broom] of destruction. Then shall the riches of the Gentiles be consecrated to the Mormonites; they shall have lands and cattle in abundance, and shall possess the gold and silver, and all the treasures of their enemies (*Mormonism Unveiled*, 1834, E.D. Howe, p. 180).

Sinful men have always been more interested in earthly wealth than in heavenly treasures, but especially if a promise of Paradise is part of the package.

• • •

May I recommend:

No Man Knows My History—The Life of Joseph Smith
by Fawn M. Brodie (499 pages)
Alfred A. Knopf, Publisher.

Chapter Three

What Mormons Believe

I. God
II. Creation
    A. Intelligence
    B. The Spirit world
        1. War in heaven
        2. Man reaps on earth what he sowed in the preexistence
III. Earth
    A. Adam and the fall
    B. Jesus, the Jehovah of the Old Testament
    C. The birth and life of Christ
    D. The atonement of Christ
    E. Temple ordinances
        1. Celestial marriages
        2. Endowments
        3. Sealings
        4. Vicarious ordinances
IV. The Future
    A. Paradise
    B. Spirit prison—hell
    C. Millennium
    D. Judgment

   E. Heaven
       1. Celestial kingdom
       2. Terrestrial kingdom
       3. Telestial kingdom
   F. Second death

To be an effective witness to the Mormons, you need to learn what they believe before you talk to them. I used to think that Mormonism was merely a corrupted form of Christianity. However, after talking to Mormons and studying Mormonism in depth, I soon realized that Mormonism is vastly different from true Christianity. Yet Mormons have been able to convince people that Mormonism is "Christianity plus," because they use parts of the Bible and many of the same terms that Bible-believing Christians use. As we look at what Mormons believe, however, it will quickly become evident that Mormonism diverges drastically from Biblical Christianity.

• • •

I. GOD. One proven scientific fact is that water will not rise higher than its source. Likewise, no religion can rise higher than its concept of God. The god of the Mormons is not the God of the Bible, but is a fabrication born in the mind of Joseph Smith.

The Mormon standard work *Doctrine and Covenants* states in section 130, verse 22:

> The Father has a body of flesh and bones as tangible as man's; the Son also; but the Holy Ghost has not a body of flesh and bones, but is a personage of Spirit. Were it not so, the Holy Ghost could not dwell in us.

The LDS Church teaches that God was initially a spirit person; he then was born on another planet—Kolob—and there received a body. In that physical state he was sinful, just like any other person. However, he progressed and became a god, and is still continuing to progress. It further teaches that this god has a body of flesh and bone; that he has many wives, with physical bodies, who give birth to spirit children through physical relationships; that later on these spirit children are born into our world and take on physical bodies. At that time these children can embark on their own road to exaltation—that is, can also become gods—and thus repeat the process all over again. The LDS Church teaches that every man is a "god" in embryo. Because this foundational doctrine of godhood is fallacious, it is only natural that the superstructure of Mormonism is specious. For this reason, it is essential to understand the Mormon concept of God.

Mormons begin with man rather than God. The words of Joseph Smith give us a clear understanding of the god of the Mormons. He made the following statement in 1844 during the funeral sermon for Mr. King Follett, a citizen of Nauvoo, Illinois:

> In order to understand the subject of the dead, it is necessary we should understand the character and being of God and how he came to be so. I am going to tell you how God came to be God. We have imagined and supposed that God was God from all eternity. I will refute that idea, and take away the veil, so that you may see. . . . Here, then, is eternal life—to know the only wise and true God; and you have got to learn how to be gods yourselves, and to be kings and priests to God, the same as all gods have done before you, namely, by going from one small degree to another, and from a small capacity to a great one; from grace to grace, from exaltation to exaltation, until you attain to the resurrection of the dead, and are able to dwell in everlasting burnings, and to sit in glory, as do those who sit enthroned in everlasting power. . . . God himself was once as we are now, and is an exalted man, and sits enthroned in yonder heavens! . . . if you were to see him today, you would see him like a man in form—like yourselves in all the person, image, and very form as a man; for Adam was created in the very fashion, image and likeness of God, and received instruction from, and

walked, talked and conversed with him, as one man talks and communes with another. (Conference Minutes of April 1844, *Times and Seasons*, Vol. 5, pp. 612–17, and *Mormon Doctrine*, p. 321).

Mormon chronicler Bruce R. McConkie further informs us:

"Every man who reigns in celestial glory is a god to his dominions," the Prophet said (*Teachings*, p. 374). Hence, the Father, who shall continue to all eternity as the God of exalted beings, is a God of Gods. Further, as the Prophet also taught, there is "a God above the Father of our Lord Jesus Christ. . . . If Jesus Christ was the Son of God, and John discovered that God the Father of Jesus Christ had a Father, you may suppose that he had a Father also. Where was there ever a son without a father? . . . Hence if Jesus had a Father, can we not believe that he had a Father also?" (*Teachings*, pp. 370, 373). In this way both the Father and the Son, as also all exalted beings, are now or in due course will become Gods of Gods (*Teachings*, pp. 342–376). (*Mormon Doctrine*, pp. 322–23).

It is plain to see that the god(s) of the Mormons is not the everlasting, unchanging, true and living God of the Bible. Mormons believe in a long succession of men who have progressed and become gods. However, they nowhere explain how the "first" man arrived on earth to begin working for his own exaltation! The Mormons think that if they simply declare that the beginning was many millions of years ago, then they do not have to face the problem of how and where everything got its start.

Orson Hyde, an early Mormon writer, tells us how the god of the Mormons gets his information:

. . . I can speak to the servant of a king when I cannot speak to the king himself. I could approach the lower orders of his subjects when I might not approach the higher circle. If men reject the administration of angels, and will not believe in their existence, nor regard their words, I do not know how they will ever obtain access to the king. If they will not acknowledge his ministers, I do not know how they are going to speak to the king himself. Have angels anything to do with what will take place in the last days? He makes His angels ministering spirits, and they are sent forth to minister for them who shall be heirs of salvation. The Lord is everywhere present by His ministering angels, just like any other ruler, monarch or king, who has ministers everywhere throughout His dominions; and God's ministers are everywhere; He has servants tabernacled in flesh on earth, and they are going through the land in every direction, and God is present everywhere with them; and He knows everything. How? When His angels and ministers tell Him of it, like any other ruler. I have been at some of the prayer circles and meetings in the sectarian world, and heard their pious ministers say, 'Come, sinner, bow to the yoke of Christ; behold the guardian angel standing waiting to be the honored agent to carry the news to heaven, that one more soul is converted.' If God knows it already, what is the use of angels to carry the intelligence? God knows everything through His agents, or servants, and that is the way He is everywhere present (*Journal of Discourses*, Vol. 2, page 64).

• • •

II. CREATION. Mormons do not believe in an original creation as found in the Bible. They teach that matter is "eternal." They do not believe that God created the world but teach that it was just organized out of existing matter. They say that God called together the gods and sat in grand council to bring forth the world and that it was "organized" into being. They believe that Christ, who was the first-born spirit child of God, had the main responsibility for organizing the world but was aided by Adam, Enoch, Noah, Abraham, Moses, Peter, James, John, *Joseph Smith*, and many other "noble and great" ones while in the spirit world.

• •

A. INTELLIGENCE. The LDS Church teaches that everything first existed as spirit elements (including man) which they call "intelligence." They teach that this "spirit element" is eternal, and therefore never had a beginning. As a spirit element, man had a conscious existence where he knew the laws, good and evil, love and hate, truth and error. They do not say how long man existed in this state, but they believe it was a long time. The Church says that all knowledge of this first existence was wiped away when this "spirit element" entered the second stage known as the "spirit world," so this is the reason no one remembers being in that state. (I don't understand how *they* know about this "intelligence" since no one remembers it—and no hint of such a condition is found in the Bible or *The Book of Mormon*.)

· ·

B. THE SPIRIT WORLD. In this second state, known as the "spirit world," the LDS Church believes that the "spirit element" or "intelligence" takes on a "spirit body" and becomes a "spirit person." Here is some more of its double-talk. While saying that God's many wives conceive and give birth to spirit children through physical relations (which takes a period of time, but the length of gestation is unstated), it contradicts itself by saying this "spirit child" in not actually a new creation but just one of the beings in the "intelligence existence" which came into the "spirit world" and began a new existence. (Of course, since it believes that all the knowledge and experience gained in the previous world was forgotten, it maintains that the education process has to begin all over again. I don't know why these spirits didn't just keep the knowledge they had from the previous existence and then add on to it!)

It teaches that in this "spirit world" there are many meetings, conferences, councils, and schooling sessions held by God and his spirit offspring, thus enabling the spirits to mature. The spirit bodies were subject to the provisions of the laws ordained for their government. The spirits had power to obey or disobey and to progress in one field or another.

In Mormon writings we have the following statement about the conditions in this "spirit world."

The preexistent life was thus a period—undoubtedly an infinitely long one—of probation, progression and schooling. The spirit hosts were taught and given experiences in various administrative capacities. Some exercised their agency and conformed to laws and became "noble and great"; these were foreordained before their natural births to perform great missions for the Lord in this life (*Mormon Doctrine*, p. 590).

As for the other forms of life in the spirit world, Bruce R. McConkie makes the following statement:

Animals, fowls, fishes, plants, and all forms of life were first created as distinct spirit entities in preexistence before they were created "naturally upon the face of the earth." That is, they lived as spirit entities before coming to this earth; they were spirit animals, spirit birds, and so forth (Moses 3:1–9). Each spirit creation had the same form as to outward appearance as it now has in mortality—"the spirit of man," the revelation specifies, being in the likeness of his person, as also the spirit of the beasts, and every other creature which God created (*Mormon Doctrine*, p. 750).

It is interesting to note that Mormons teach that in the spirit world, man and Jesus were of the same order of being, of the same race, nature and essence. They say that Jesus was the first-born spirit child of the God of this universe and that every man or woman is as much deity as Jesus Christ, because all are spirit-born children of God. They also teach that Satan was one of the spirit-born children of God, thus making Jesus and Satan spiritual brothers.

·

1. WAR IN HEAVEN. Near the end of the period of probation in the spirit world when God was going to send these spirits to earth so they could receive mortal bodies (Mormons claim these bodies are necessary to the process of exaltation), he called a council of the gods. One question that came up concerned "the

redemption of the world." Bruce McConkie tells us about these councils:

> There were many meetings, conferences, councils, and schooling sessions held among the Gods and their spirit offspring in preexistence. Among other things, at these various assemblages, plans were made for the creation and peopling of this earth and for the redemption and salvation of the offspring of Deity. The spirit children of the Father were then taught the terms and conditions of the plan of salvation and were given opportunity to accept or reject the Father's proposals.... Ordinarily, perhaps, when the saints speak of the council of heaven, they have in mind the solemn session (at which, apparently, all of the preexistent hosts were present) when the Father made formal announcement of his plan of redemption and salvation. It was then explained that his spirit children would go down to earth, gain bodies of flesh and blood, be tried and tested in all things, and have opportunity by obedience to come back again to the Eternal Presence. It was then explained that one of the spirit children of the Father would be chosen to be the Redeemer and work out the infinite and eternal atonement. And it was then that the Father sent forth the call which said in substance and effect: Whom shall I send to be my Son in mortality? Who will go down, be born with life himself, and work out the great atoning sacrifice by which immortality will come to all men and eternal life be assured to the obedient?
>
> Two mighty spirits answered the call and volunteered their service. Christ said, in effect: Here am I, send me: I will be thy Son; I will follow thy plan; and "thy will be done, and the glory be thine forever." Lucifer sought to amend the plan of the Father to change the proffered terms of salvation. "Behold, here am I, send me," he said, "I will be thy son [sic], and I will redeem all mankind, that one soul shall not be lost, and surely I will do it; wherefore give me thine honor" (Moses 4:1–4). When the Father said, "I will send the first," then Lucifer was angry, kept not his first estate, rebelled, and he and one-third of the host of heaven were cast out down to the earth to become the devil and his angels (*Mormon Doctrine*, pp. 163–64).

•

2. MAN REAPS ON EARTH WHAT HE SOWED IN THE PREEXISTENCE.

Mormons teach that while man was in the spirit world, he went through a time of testing. If a person was obedient and valiant in the spirit world, he was assured of being born into a good family who lived in a powerful nation. If he was very good, he would be born into a white Mormon family. If he was less valiant, he would be born with darker skin, and the least valiant would be born with black skin. Bruce McConkie writes:

> In the preexistent eternity various degrees of valiance and devotion to the truth were exhibited by different groups of our Father's spirit offspring. One-third of the spirit hosts of heaven came out in open rebellion and were cast out without bodies, becoming the devil and his angels. . . . Of the two-thirds who followed Christ, however, some were more valiant than others. . . . Those who were less valiant in preexistence and who thereby had certain spiritual restrictions imposed upon them during mortality are known to us as Negroes. Such spirits are sent to earth through the lineage of Cain, the mark put upon him for his rebellion against God and his murder of Abel being a black skin (Moses 5:16–41; 7:8, 12, 22). Noah's son Ham married Egyptus, a descendant of Cain, thus preserving the Negro lineage through the flood (Abraham 1:20–27) (*Mormon Doctrine*, pp. 526–27).

The Book of Mormon states that when people committed certain sins their skin was supposed to become darker, so the mention of Cain's skin darkening in this quote is fully consistent with *The Book of Mormon*.

Bruce McConkie continues:

> Negroes in this life are denied the priesthood, under no circumstances can they hold this delegation of authority from the Almighty (Abraham 1:20–27). The gospel message is not carried

affirmatively to them (Moses 7:8,12, 22)*. . . . The present status of the Negro rests purely and simply on the foundation of preexistence. Along with all races and peoples he is receiving here what he merits as a result of the long premortal probation in the presence of the Lord. . . .

The Negroes are not equal with other races where the receipt of certain spiritual blessings is concerned, particularly the priesthood and the temple blessings that flow therefrom, but this inequality is not of man's origin. It is the Lord's doing, is based on his eternal laws of justice, and grows out of the lack of spiritual valiance of those concerned in their first estate (*Mormon Doctrine*, pp. 527–28).

The black man is allowed to have a body, but until June 1978 he was not eligible to hold office in the Mormon church. The Mormons believe that holding an office is necessary for exaltation. (Women still are not able to hold any of the priesthoods.)

• • •

III. EARTH. In the third realm of existence, man is on the Earth—the planet which we inhabit. Here he obtains a physical body and undergoes the probation of mortality. The LDS Church teaches that a physical body is absolutely necessary for exaltation (becoming a god).

• •

A. ADAM AND THE FALL. From McConkie we learn what the Mormons teach about Adam and the fall:

By his diligence and obedience there [in the preexistent world], as one of the spirit sons of God, he attained a stature and power second only to that of Christ, the Firstborn. None of all the billions of our Father's children equaled him in intelligence and might, save Jesus only. He sat in the council of the gods in the planning of the creation of this earth, and then, under Christ participated

* The Book of Abraham and the Book of Moses are two of the five divisions of *The Pearl of Great Price*, a Mormon standard work.

in the creative enterprise (Abraham 3:22–26). He was foreordained to come to earth as the father of the human race, and when Lucifer and one-third of the hosts of heaven rebelled, Adam (with the exalted title of Michael the Archangel) led the hosts of the righteous in the war in heaven (Revelation 12:7–9). . . . Adam's great part in the plan of redemption was to fall from the immortal state in which he first existed on earth and thus bring mortality and death into the world. This he did, bringing temporal and spiritual death into the world, from the effects of which death the atonement of Christ was foreordained as a ransom. After the fall, Adam and Eve became parents of all living. . . . Father Adam was one of the most noble and intelligent characters who ever lived. He began his earthly life as a son of God, endowed with the talents and abilities gained through diligence and obedience in preexistence. He is the head of all gospel dispensations, the presiding high priest (under Christ) over all the earth: presiding over all the spirits destined to inhabit this earth; holds the keys of salvation over all the earth; and will reign as Michael, our prince, to all eternity (*Mormon Doctrine*, pp. 16–17).

Mormons teach that when Adam fell, he went in the right direction. Adam and Eve were able to have physical children because of the fall and then make physical bodies available for the preexistent spirits. They say that Adam was given two conflicting commandments. One was, "Be fruitful, and multiply, and replenish the earth" (Genesis 1:28). The other was, "But of the tree of the knowledge of good and evil, thou shalt not eat of it" (Genesis 2:17). Adam would not have become mortal and could not have had children if he had obeyed God's command not to partake of the tree of good and evil. Since the preexistent spirits needed bodies to progress on the road to exaltation, Adam's sin is considered to be good. In fact, they say that Adam's sin was necessary, so "Adam fell that man might be."

The LDS Church teaches that when Adam and Eve were first created they were not fully human beings and in that state could not produce children, but after the fall they became human and could produce bodies so that the spirits in the "spirit world" could come down and dwell in these physical bodies, which was another step in the possibility of becoming a god.

• •

B. JESUS THE JEHOVAH OF THE OLD TESTAMENT. Mormons believe that before Jesus received a body on this earth two thousand years ago that he was Jehovah during the Old Testament times and was the one who ruled the Earth. However, they teach that the spirits born in the "spirit world" must have a physical body before they can begin to progress on the road of becoming a god. But Jesus had not yet received a physical body in the Old Testament period, so how could he be Jehovah of the O.T. who is clearly recognized as God! Jesus was simply a spirit! The Mormons I have talked to have never been able to explain this paradox.

• •

C. THE BIRTH AND LIFE OF JESUS CHRIST. Mormonism teaches that Jesus is the *literal* Son of God because he was born as a result of physical relations between God and Mary. (Remember, the Mormon's god has a physical body.) Bruce McConkie writes:

> God the Father is a perfected, glorified, holy Man, an immortal Personage. And Christ was born into the world as the literal Son of this Holy Being; he was born in the same personal, real, and literal sense that any mortal son is born to a mortal father. There is nothing figurative about his paternity; he was begotten, conceived and born in the normal and natural course of events, for he is the Son of God, and that designation means what it says (*Mormon Doctrine*, p. 742).

Mormons claim that Mary was Joseph's wife only while here on earth and state that in eternity Mary will be one of God's wives. They deny the virgin birth of Christ through the power of the Holy Spirit. When they talk about the virgin birth, they mean that Jesus was born of direct relations between the Father and Mary, not by the Holy Spirit.

In spite of the fact that God is supposed to be the Father of Jesus, they do not believe that Christ was perfect at the time of his birth. They teach that he received grace for grace, and that he continued to receive more grace until he received a fullness.

We need to remember that the Mormons think that Christ is not superior to the average man. They teach that man can be exalted to the same position as Christ.

Another of the blasphemous teachings of the Mormon church is that Jesus was a polygamist. They teach that it was Jesus who was married at the wedding in Cana of Galilee. They say Mary, Martha, Mary Magdalene, and others were his wives and that he begot children.

In two talks given by Orson Hyde, the Mormon belief is explained:

> When does it say the Savior was married? . . . Gentlemen, that is as plain as the translators, or different councils over this Scripture, dare allow it to go to the world, but the thing is there; it is told; Jesus was the bridegroom at the marriage of Cana of Galilee [John 2:1–11], and he told them what to do. . . . Well, then, he shall see his seed, and who shall declare his generation, for he was cut off from the earth? I shall say here, that before the Savior died, he looked upon his own natural children, as we look upon ours; he saw his seed, and immediately afterwards he was cut off from the earth; but who shall declare his generation? (*Journal of Discourses*, Vol. 2, page 82).

> I discovered that some of the Eastern papers represent me as a great blasphemer, because I said, in my lecture on Marriage, at our last Conference, that Jesus Christ was married at Cana of Galilee, that Mary, Martha, and others were his wives, and that he

begat children.

All that I have to say in reply to that charge is this—they worship a Savior that is too pure and holy to fulfill the commands of his Father. I worship one that is just pure and holy enough "to fulfill all righteousness"; . . . Startle not at this! for even the Father himself honored that law by coming down to Mary, without a natural body, and begetting a son; and if Jesus begat children, he only "did that which he had seen his Father do" (*Journal of Discourses*, Vol. 2, page 210).

• •

D. THE ATONEMENT OF CHRIST. Mormons believe that there are two kinds of salvation—unconditional salvation and individual salvation. They teach that Christ died for all the sins we inherited from Adam, therefore salvation is unconditional in that all men are saved from eternal death by grace, without works. (Ephesians 2:8–9 can't be used effectively with a Mormon because he believes that unconditional salvation—resurrection of the physical body—is by grace.) Thus all men will be resurrected and go into one of the three heavens.

Beyond unconditional salvation, there is individual salvation which man has to work for. They say that though Christ died for the sins we repent of, that is still not enough. The Mormon concept of salvation can be illustrated by a person who has fallen into a deep pit with no way for him to get out. Christ came along and provided a ladder so that he can climb out of the pit. Christ does not give anyone this ladder directly. He has committed it to the Mormon church and they give it to their followers. However, you do not just climb up the ladder and get out of the pit. The rungs are made of certain stipulations for exaltation imposed by the Mormon church. Mormonism teaches that a person can climb up but he falls back when he is disobedient. If a person does not get to the top (the celestial kingdom, where he becomes a god), he can go to the terrestrial or telestial kingdom. No one has to stay at the bottom, which is the place of the second death.

The LDS Church might talk a lot about Christ, but in reality he plays no part in their personal salvation. A person can only get to the celestial kingdom and have a chance to become a god if he is a member of the LDS Church. (It is interesting to note that by their own admission only 5% of the Mormons have taken part in the many necessary steps to becoming a god, even if it were possible. Take another look at the list of requirements on page 68.) The LSD church maintains that a person must believe that Joseph Smith was a true prophet of God and needs his permission before he can enter into the celestial kingdom.

· ·

E. TEMPLE ORDINANCES. For a Christian, the church is a meeting place where he can worship the Lord and have fellowship with other Christians. Mormons also have churches (known as "wards") for their weekly meetings. Their temples, however, are not meeting places similar to Christian church buildings. They say:

> Temples are holy sanctuaries wherein sacred ordinances, rites, and ceremonies are performed which pertain to salvation and exaltation in the kingdom of God (*Mormon Doctrine*, p. 779).

The temple is a necessity because they believe that certain ordinances are only effective when performed in the temple. They say:

> Certain gospel ordinances are of such a sacred and holy nature that the Lord authorizes their performance only in holy sanctuaries prepared and dedicated for that very purpose. Except in circumstances of great poverty and distress, these ordinances can be performed only in temples, and hence they are commonly called temple ordinances. Baptism for the dead, an ordinance opening the door to the celestial kingdom to worthy persons not privileged to undergo gospel schooling while in mortality, is a temple

ordinance, an ordinance of salvation. All other temple ordinances—washings, anointings, endowments, sealings—pertain to exaltation within the celestial kingdom. Celestial marriage is the gate which puts men on the path leading to the highest of three heavens within the celestial world (*Mormon Doctrine*, p. 779).

A look at some of these ordinances will help in understanding the complicated Mormon teaching as to how one can be exalted. Of course, none of this is found in the Bible or even in *The Book of Mormon*. It is an unfair system, because those who live a great distance from a temple have to put forth a greater effort and spend more than those who live close to a temple.

•

1. CELESTIAL MARRIAGES. Mormons teach that people can live as families in the celestial kingdom. They hold that civil and church marriages are only for this life, but marriages performed or later solemnized in the temple will last for eternity. They state:

> Marriages performed in the temples for time and eternity, by virtue of the sealing keys restored by Elijah, are called "celestial marriages." The participating parties become husband and wife in this mortal life, and if after their marriage they keep all the terms and conditions of this order of the priesthood, they continue on as husband and wife in the celestial kingdom of God. If the family unit continues, they by virtue of that fact, the members of the family, have gained eternal life (exaltation), the greatest of all the gifts of God, for by definition exaltation consists in the continuation of the family unit in eternity (*Mormon Doctrine*, p. 117).

If this teaching is true it presents a number of major problems for the Mormons. For example, when children get married, they start new families of their own. Mormon teaching is that each man can become a god and begin a new universe with his wives. If parents' sons have this privilege of becoming gods with their own universes, then how can they live together when they are in different universes?

·

2. ENDOWMENTS. This is a Mormon catechetical term which encompasses a number of prescribed duties and vows pertaining to covenants and obligations, with a blessing promised to those individuals who faithfully observe the conditions. Certain special, spiritual blessings are given worthy and faithful saints in the temples and these are called "endowments" because in and through them the recipients are endowed with power from on high. They receive an education relative to the Lord's purposes and plans in the creation and peopling of the earth and are taught the things that must be done by man in order to gain exaltation in the world to come (*Mormon Doctrine*, pp. 226–27).

·

3. SEALINGS. Mormons believe that relationships must be solemnized in the temple if they are to exist in the future kingdom. They write: "Those ordinances performed in the temple whereby husbands and wives are sealed together in the marriage union for time and eternity, and whereby children are sealed eternally to parents, are commonly referred to as 'sealings'" (*Mormon Doctrine*, p. 684).

·

4. VICARIOUS ORDINANCES. An important Mormon teaching is that the living are able to observe certain ordinances that will help their dead ancestors and others to achieve exaltation. The following statement explains this teaching:

> Salvation itself is based on the vicarious atoning sacrifice of Christ. Through his suffering, death, and resurrection immortality comes to all men and eternal life to those who obey the full gospel law. He acted on man's behalf, that is, vicariously, paying the penalty for our sins on condition of repentance, ransoming us from the effects of Adam's fall. In conformity with this pattern of

vicarious service, the gospel law enables worthy members of the Church to act on behalf of their dead ancestors in the performance of the ordinances of salvation and exaltation. Baptism is essential to salvation in the celestial kingdom, endowments and sealings to an exaltation therein. The living saints, acting on a proxy basis, perform these ordinances for and on behalf of those who have died and who did not have an opportunity while in this life to receive the ordinances personally (*Mormon Doctrine*, p. 822).

· · ·

IV. THE FUTURE. The Mormons have some unusual teachings as to what happens after this earthly life is over.

· ·

A. PARADISE. Mormons teach that at the time of death, the body goes into the grave to await the resurrection and the soul goes into either "paradise" or "spirit prison"—hell. Paradise is the abode of the righteous who have been baptized into the Mormon church and who have been faithful to the Mormon teachings. Thus, only Mormons will enter paradise. During this time, the righteous spirits (Mormons) will go and preach the Mormon gospel to other spirits, those imprisoned in hell. Paradise is described as follows:

Life and work and activity all continue in the spirit world. Men have the same talents and intelligence there which they had in this life. They possess the same attitudes, inclinations, and feelings there which they had in this life. They believe the same things, as far as eternal truths are concerned; they continue, in effect, to walk in the same path they were following in this life. . . . The great work in the world of spirits is the preaching of the gospel to those who are imprisoned by sin and false traditions. The faithful elders who depart this life continue their labors for the salvation of their brethren in the spirit world. Those who would have received the gospel in this life, if the opportunity had come to them, will repent and receive it in the next life and will thereby become heirs of salvation (*Mormon Doctrine*, pp. 762–63).

• •

B. SPIRIT PRISON—HELL. Anyone who was not a faithful Mormon will go to this place after death and will be a disembodied spirit. In spirit prison—hell—they will pay for their own sins. However, it is only a temporary place until the second resurrection. When explaining this spirit prison Mormons say:

> That part of the spirit world inhabited by wicked spirits who are awaiting the eventual day of their resurrection is called "hell." Between their death and resurrection, these souls of the wicked are cast out into outer darkness, into the gloomy depression of sheol, into the Hades of waiting wicked spirits, into hell. There they suffer the torments of the damned; there they welter in the vengeance of eternal fire; there is found weeping and wailing and gnashing of teeth; there the fiery indignation of the wrath of God is poured out upon the wicked (*Mormon Doctrine*, p. 349).

> Now that the righteous spirits in paradise have been commissioned to carry the message of salvation to the wicked spirits in hell, there is a certain amount of mingling together of the good and bad spirits. Repentance opens the prison doors to the spirits in hell; it enables those bound with the chains of hell to free themselves from darkness, unbelief, ignorance, and sin. As rapidly as they can overcome these obstacles—gain light, believe truth, acquire intelligence, cast off sin, and break the chains of hell—they can leave the hell that imprisons them and dwell with the righteous in the peace of paradise (*Mormon Doctrine*, p. 775).

The Mormon practice of "baptism for the dead" comes in at this point. They believe that if they are baptized in a Mormon temple for someone who did not hear the Mormon gospel while here on earth, it will enable that person to respond to the gospel heard in the spirit prison after death. When the wicked spirits repent, they leave their prison—hell—and join the righteous in paradise. Mormon writings say:

Based on the eternal principle of vicarious service, the Lord has ordained "baptism for the dead" as the means whereby all his worthy children of all ages can become heirs of salvation in his kingdom. Baptism is the gate to the celestial kingdom. . . . Obviously, during the frequent periods of apostate darkness when the gospel light does not shine, and also in those geographical areas where legal administrators are not found, hosts of people live and die without ever entering in at the gate of baptism so as to be on the path leading to eternal life. For them a just God has ordained baptism for the dead, a vicarious-proxy labor (*Mormon Doctrine*, p. 73).

However, this work of "baptism for the dead" must be recorded properly if it is to be effective. In the early days of Mormonism hundreds were baptized for the dead, but the baptisms were not recorded; they had to be done a second time. Mormons spend millions of dollars on genealogical research in order to find the names of those who have died without being baptized into the Mormon church. More than 5 billion names are on file, to which Mormons may refer when seeking names of people for whom they can do proxy baptism. The names of those who have been given proxy baptisms are microfilmed and stored in a huge vault in Utah. In 1976 Bruce R. McConkie wrote:

Before vicarious ordinances of salvation and exaltation may be performed for those who have died without a knowledge of the gospel, but who presumably would have received it had the opportunity come to them, they must be accurately and properly identified. Hence, "genealogical research" is required. To aid its members in intelligent and effective research, the Church maintains in Salt Lake City one of the world's greatest "genealogical societies." Much of the genealogical source material of various nations of the earth has been or is being microfilmed by this society; millions of dollars is being spent; and a reservoir of hundreds of millions of names and other data about people who lived in past generations is available for study (*Mormon Doctrine*, pp. 308-9).

Baptism for a dead person does not mean that person will automatically respond to the Mormon gospel in the spirit prison. The individual is free to receive or reject the message. It is also interesting to note that males can only be baptized for males, and females can only be baptized for females. Since proxy baptism gives people hope that their dead loved ones will go to heaven, it helps Mormons in their proselytizing.

•   •

C. THE MILLENNIUM. Mormons teach that the earth is passing through a temporal existence of seven millenniums (7000 years). From the fall of Adam until the second coming of Christ, which ushers in the final millennium, is a period of 6000 years. The Mormons living upon the earth at Christ's return and those resurrected from paradise in the first resurrection will enter into the millennial kingdom. Also some nonmembers of the LDS Church will enter the millennium. (They believe that the wicked on earth at this time will be destroyed and will be sent to the spirit prison—hell.) They make the following statement:

> Since all who are living at least a terrestrial law—the law of honesty, uprightness, and integrity—will be able to abide the day of our Lord's coming, there will be nonmembers of the Church on earth during the millennium. Honest and upright people who have been deceived by the false religions and false philosophies of the world will not have their free agency abridged. They will continue to believe their false doctrines until they voluntarily elect to receive gospel light (*Mormon Doctrine*, pp. 498–99).

However, they believe that all nonmembers of the LDS Church that go into the millennium will be converted to the Mormon gospel during this time. They describe conditions upon the earth during the millennium as follows:

> Men in that day will still be mortal; children will be born to

them; spirits coming into the physical or natural bodies born in that day will then go through their mortal probation as we are now going through ours. Children will be born, grow up, marry, advance to old age, and pass through the equivalent of death. Crops will be planted, harvested, and eaten; industries will be expanded, cities built, and education fostered; men will continue to care for their own needs, handle their own affairs, and enjoy the full endowment of free agency (*Mormon Doctrine*, p. 497).

Mormons believe that the temple ordinances will continue during the millennium. They say that genealogical records that were unknown to man upon the earth will become available, so that baptism for the dead can be accelerated. The doctrine of polygamy is a very important part of their religion even though the Mormons don't like to talk about it: they believe that polygamy will be reinstated during the millennium.

• •

D. JUDGMENT. The second resurrection will follow the millennium. Mormons teach that people who are alive at the end of the millennium and those from the spirit prison—hell—who have been raised in the second resurrection and given a body, will stand before God to be judged according to their works and merit. They will be assigned to one of the three kingdoms.

Joseph Fielding Smith, the tenth president of the Mormon church, wrote:

ALL SAVED EXCEPT SONS OF PERDITION. It is a very pleasing and consoling thing to know that the Lord will save all of his children, excepting the very few who willfully rebel against him. When his children have paid the penalty of their transgressions, they shall come forth from the clutches of the second death to receive a place somewhere in the great heavenly kingdoms, which are prepared for them with their several glories and degrees of salvation. It is the purpose of the Almighty to save all mankind, and all will enter into his kingdoms in some degree of glory, except sons of perdition who sin beyond the power of repentance and redemption, and therefore cannot receive forgiveness of sins. All the rest shall be saved but not all with the same degree of glory or exaltation. Every man will be judged according to his works, his opportunities for receiving the truth, and the intent of his heart (*Doctrines of Salvation*, Vol. II, p. 21).

· · ·

E. HEAVEN. Mormons believe that all people (except the sons of perdition) will go to heaven. In their heaven, there are three degrees of glory or three kingdoms to which man will go after the judgment. They try to use the Bible to prove their mistaken idea of heaven, and quote 1 Corinthians 15:39–42 which says: "All flesh is not the same flesh: but there is one kind of flesh of men, another flesh of beasts, another of fishes, another of birds. There are also celestial bodies, and bodies terrestrial: but the glory of the celestial is one, and the glory of the terrestrial is another. There is one glory of the sun, and another glory of the moon, and another glory of the stars: for one star differeth from another star in glory. So also is the resurrection of the dead. It is sown in corruption; it is raised in incorruption." Joseph Smith taught that the sun represents the highest kingdom, which he called the "celestial kingdom." The moon stands for the second kingdom known as the "terrestrial kingdom." The lowest of the three is represented by the stars and is the "telestial kingdom." ("Telestial" is a word made up by Joseph Smith and is not found in the English dictionary.)

Concerning this teaching, Bruce R. McConkie states:

Contrary to the views found in the uninspired teachings and creeds of modern Christendom, there are in eternity kingdoms of glory to which all resurrected persons (except the sons of perdition) will eventually go. These are named: celestial, terrestrial, and telestial—the glory of each being beyond mortal comprehension. However, only the celestial kingdom is the kingdom of God where the faithful saints will gain their eternal inheritance. All who fall short of the glory of eternal life will in greater or lesser degree be damned (even though they dwell in a kingdom of glory), for their eternal progress will be limited, and they can never go on to an eternal fullness in the Father's presence. Rewards granted individuals in eternity will vary between and within kingdoms. Only those who are sealed in the new and everlasting covenant will attain the highest of three heavens within the celestial kingdom (*Mormon Doctrine*, p. 420).

•

1. CELESTIAL KINGDOM. This kingdom is reserved only for Mormons, but not all Mormons will go there. Since their system depends upon ordinances and works which determine their future glory, no Mormon can be sure which kingdom he will enter. The celestial kingdom is itself divided into three realms. The highest of the three is for Mormons who have been married in the temple and who have lived lives worthy of celestial glory, enabling them to go on to exaltation. Mormons teach that this group will live as families and continue to have children, which they define as "eternal life." On this subject, Mormon authorities write:

Except a man and his wife enter into an everlasting covenant and be married for eternity, while in this probation, by the power and authority of the holy priesthood, they will cease to increase when they die; that is, they will not have children after the resurrection. Then with reference to those who have been properly sealed in marriage and who have thereafter endured in righteousness until their callings and elections were made sure by revelation . . . will continue to increase and have children in the celestial glory (*Mormon Doctrine*, p. 238).

Mormons teach that those who go into the highest degree of glory in the celestial kingdom will be able to progress until they become gods. They write:

That exaltation which the saints of all ages have so devoutly sought is "godhood" itself. Godhood is to have the character, possess the attributes, and enjoy the perfections which the Father has. It is to do what he does, have the powers resident in him, and live as he lives, having eternal increase. . . . They are gods (*Mormon Doctrine*, p. 321).

The Father has promised us that through our faithfulness we shall be blessed with the fullness of his kingdom. . . . To become like him we must have all the powers of godhood; thus a man and his wife when glorified will have spirit children who eventually will go on an earth like this one we are on and pass through the same kind of experience, being subject to mortal conditions, and if faithful, then they also will receive the fullness of exaltation and partake of the same blessings. There is no end to this development: it will go on forever. We will become gods and have jurisdiction over worlds, and these worlds will be peopled by our own offspring. We will have an endless eternity for this (*Doctrines of Salvation*, Vol. II, p. 48).

And what about the people that go into the lower ranks of the celestial kingdom? They too will be able to live as families, even though they cannot become gods themselves.

·

2. TERRESTRIAL KINGDOM. Mormons teach that those who go into this kingdom were good people who rejected the Mormon beliefs while on the earth. They say that in this kingdom they will have the presence of the Son, but not the Father. (This shows they believe that Jesus Christ is inferior to God the Father.) Those who enter the terrestrial kingdom will not be able to marry or live as families, nor will they be able to progress.

Bruce R. McConkie informs us that:

To the "terrestrial kingdom" will go: 1. Accountable persons who die without law (and who, of course, do not accept the gospel in the spirit world under those particular circumstances which would make them heirs of the celestial kingdom); 2. Those who reject the gospel in this life and who reverse their course and accept it in the spirit world; 3. Honorable men of the earth who are blinded by the craftiness of men and who therefore do not accept and live the gospel law; and 4. Members of The Church of Jesus Christ of Latter-day Saints who have testimonies of Christ and the divinity of the great latter-day work and who are not valiant, but who are instead lukewarm in their devotion to the Church and to righteousness (*Mormon Doctrine*, p. 784).

Joseph Fielding Smith states:

Some of the functions in the celestial body will not appear in the terrestrial body, neither in the telestial body, and the power of procreation will be removed. I take it that men and women will, in these kingdoms, be just what the so-called Christian world expects us all to be—neither man nor woman, merely immortal beings having received the resurrection (*Doctrines of Salvation*, Vol. II, p. 288).

·

3. TELESTIAL KINGDOM. This is the lowest of the three kingdoms and is for those who lived "wicked lives" while they were on the earth.

Their teaching is made clear in the following statement:

Most of the adult people who have lived from the day of Adam to the present time will go to the "telestial kingdom." The inhabitants of this lower kingdom of glory will be "as innumerable as the stars in the firmament of heaven, or as the sands upon the seashore." They will be the endless hosts of people of all ages who have lived after the manner of the world; who have been carnal, sensual, and devilish; who have chosen the vain philosophies of the world rather than accept the testimony of Jesus; who have been liars and thieves, sorcerers and adulterers, blasphemers and murderers. Their number will include "all the proud, yea, and all that do wickedly" (Malachi 4:1), for all such have lived a telestial law. They shall be servants of the Most High; but where God and Christ dwell they cannot come (*Mormon Doctrine*, p. 778).

· · ·

F. SECOND DEATH. Mormons teach that Satan will enter the "second death." With Satan will be one-third of the spirits, those who followed him in his rebellion against God (the sons of perdition). They say that there will be very few humans who will go into the second death. Those humans who do go there are either those who have blasphemed against the Holy Spirit (those who leave the Mormon church and are excommunicated) or are murderers who did not shed their own blood to atone for their sins. Yes, Mormons have an odd doctrine known as "blood atonement." They teach that Christ only died for some sins, and murder is not one of them. Therefore, they maintain, if a person commits murder he will become one of the "sons of perdition" and go into the second death—unless his own blood is shed. This, then, will allow him to move up to the "telestial kingdom."

Prior to Utah's statehood, Mormon leaders would customarily cut the throat of anyone who had committed murder. Utah still permits execution by shooting. Another possible solution is for the murderer to commit suicide by cutting his throat or wrists, thus shedding his own blood.

Again we turn to Bruce R. McConkie for an explanation of their teaching on this subject:

> Lucifer is Perdition. He became such by open rebellion against the truth, a rebellion in the face of light and knowledge. Although he knew God and had been taught the provisions of the plan of salvation, he defied the Lord and sought to enthrone himself with the Lord's power (Moses 4:1–4). He thus committed the unpardonable sin. In rebellion with him were one-third of the spirit hosts of heaven. These all were thus followers (or in other words sons) of perdition. They were denied bodies, were cast out into the earth, and thus came the devils and his angels—a great host of

"sons of perdition."

Those in this life who gain a perfect knowledge of the divinity of the gospel course, a knowledge that comes only by revelation from the Holy Ghost, and who then link themselves with Lucifer and come out in open rebellion, also become sons of perdition. Their destiny, following their resurrection, is to be cast out with the devil and his angels, to inherit the same kingdom in a state where "the worm dieth not, and the fire is not quenched" (*Mormon Doctrine*, p. 476).

The Christian who is familiar with what the Bible teaches will soon recognize that Mormon doctrine is not Biblical nor is it Christian. Rather, much of it is high-flying speculation that deserves to be lumped with the jumble of early Christian heresies known as "Gnosticism." Paul's counsel to Timothy seems appropriate: "Neither give heed to fables and endless genealogies, which minister questions, rather than godly edifying" (1 Timothy 1:4).

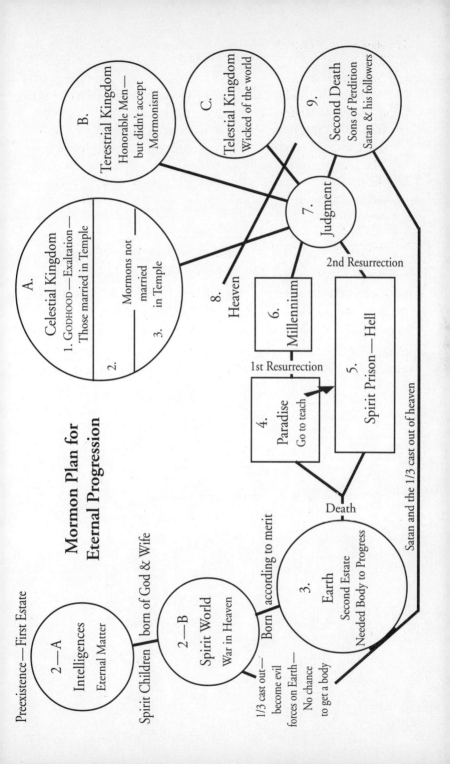

Mormon Plan for Eternal Progression

Preexistence — First Estate

2 — A
Intelligences
Eternal Matter

Spirit Children born of God & Wife

2 — B
Spirit World
War in Heaven

1/3 cast out —
become evil
forces on Earth —
No chance
to get a body

Born according to merit

3.
Earth
Second Estate
Needed Body to Progress

Death

Satan and the 1/3 cast out of heaven

4.
Paradise
Go to teach

1st Resurrection

6.
Millennium

5.
Spirit Prison — Hell

2nd Resurrection

8.
Heaven

7.
Judgment

A.
Celestial Kingdom
1. GODHOOD — Exaltation —
Those married in Temple

2.

3. Mormons not
married
in Temple

B.
Terestrial Kingdom
Honorable Men —
but didn't accept
Mormonism

C.
Telestial Kingdom
Wicked of the world

9.
Second Death
Sons of Perdition
Satan & his followers

Chapter Four

Explanation of Mormon Terms

W HEN I first started witnessing
to Mormons, I was confused because I found that we were using
the same terms but were giving them entirely different meanings. I knew that their beliefs were not the same as a born-again
Christian's beliefs—but often they would agree with what I had
said. As I continued witnessing, I gradually realized that they had
entirely different meanings for many of the common Biblical terms
with which I was familiar. As I began to understand what they
meant when they used those terms, I was able to explain the
truth more effectively. For this reason, I have listed a number of
these terms with their Mormon definitions.

• • •

1. AUTHORITY—The LDS Church teaches that God gave
Joseph Smith the authority to restore the church upon this earth.
Joseph Smith claimed that John the Baptist, Peter, James, John,
Elijah, and others appeared to him and gave him certain "keys"
which gave him the authority to "act for God" here upon earth
for the salvation of men. The authority of God that was delegated to Joseph Smith is said to be passed on from Joseph Smith
to all males who hold the priesthood. The LDS Church claims
that it is the only church that has the authority to act for God
upon this earth. It even goes so far as to say that when the presi-

dent of the Mormon church speaks, it is actually God speaking to them.

• • •

2. BAPTISM—This is an absolute necessity for Mormons. They teach that a person must be immersed by someone having the authority (that means, someone holding the proper Mormon priesthood) and it must be properly recorded in the records of the LDS Church. For Mormons, baptism serves four purposes:

a. It is for the remission of sins. In reality, this means very little, since they teach that man is basically good and so do not emphasize personal sin.

b. It admits the person to membership into the LDS Church, which they claim is the kingdom of God on earth.

c. It is the gate to the celestial kingdom of heaven (i.e., it starts a person out on the straight and narrow path which leads to eternal life).

d. It is the key that opens the door to a person's sanctification.

• • •

3. BORN AGAIN—For Mormons, being born again is a process and not an act. They say the process begins when one is baptized into the LDS Church. The next step is receiving the Holy Ghost by the laying on of hands. However, this does not guarantee that a born-again (according to the LDS definition) person will reach the celestial kingdom, which is his ultimate goal. He must also obey the ordinances and regulation of the LDS Church to continue the process of being born again.

• • •

4. DAMNATION—To the Mormon, "damnation" is the opposite of "salvation" (becoming a god). To be damned means to change the flow of eternal progression—similar to what happens when a dam is constructed in a stream and changes its flow. They stress that a dam in a stream or river does not keep the water from eventually reaching the ocean, it just changes its course.

They teach that there are four groups of damned people.

a. Those who go to the "spirit prison—hell" and suffer until the day of resurrection.

b. Those who fail to become gods but gain a place in the second or third compartment of the celestial kingdom.

c. Those who fail to enter the celestial kingdom and go to either the terrestrial or the telestial kingdom.

d. Those who become sons of perdition.

•   •   •

5. DEITY—Mormons not only believe in the deity of Christ, but they also believe in the deity of man. They say that all men are spirit-born children of God and are therefore divine.

•   •   •

6. ETERNAL LIFE—They teach that God has eternal life, and that men who became gods have the same eternal life. Men become gods and gain eternal life by their own works. They say that it is something they merit and not a gift from God.

Mormons also use this term in another sense. They teach that knowledge is eternal, so that all men have always existed in some form—intelligence, spirit children, mortal, resurrected bodies—thus saying that everyone has eternal life. It has nothing to do with salvation.

•   •   •

7. ETERNAL DEATH—This term applies to people who enter into the terrestrial and telestial kingdom after the resurrection. Mormons say that the people who go to these kingdoms will not be able to live as families, have children, or progress. It would be like a family's name dying out when there are no sons to carry on the name.

•   •   •

8. ETERNAL PUNISHMENT—To the Mormon, "eternal" is not a term used in relation to time but in relation to God. Eternal punishment is punishment that God administers. Mor-

mon doctrine teaches that any punishment from God is eternal punishment. Therefore, they do not believe in a literal everlasting (i.e., as to time) punishment.

• • •

9. GODHEAD—Mormons use this term in referring to the Father, the Son, and the Holy Ghost. They do not mean that the three persons are one God and exactly equal. They believe that there are three different gods who rule the universe. They talk about each person belonging to the Godhead. Also, they use the word to express the whole purpose of existence and the goal of every Mormon male. (Females cannot become gods.)

• • •

10. GODHOOD: HOW TO ACHIEVE IT—The Mormon system can be likened to a company with a president and many workers under him. A person enters the company at the bottom, but there is a possibility that some day he may be the president if he works hard. If a person is worthy, God will give him all the resources needed to start his own company (another universe). This person will be the president, and will have his spirit-born children who will be working their way up the ladder. In other words, the only difference between the president and a person just entering is time, experience, and intelligence. The potential to become a god is there if one is willing to work hard. The Mormon's god is only an exalted man. They teach that all males can enter into exaltation (becoming a god) by their own good works through the Mormon church system. However, "good works" means being in complete submission to the Mormon authorities (mainly paying tithe) and has nothing to do with moral character and personal holiness.

• • •

11. GOSPEL—The LDS Church's system which embraces all the laws, principles, doctrines, temple rites, ordinances, acts, powers, authorities, and keys necessary to save and exalt men in the highest heaven hereafter.

. . . .

12. HOLY GHOST—Mormons teach that the Holy Ghost is the third member of the Godhead, and that he is a personage of spirit, a spirit person, a spirit man, and a spirit entity. They do not explain these terms. They say he can be in only one place at one time, and cannot transform himself into any other form or image than that of the spirit man who he is. However, they say his power and influence can be manifest at one and the same time throughout all places.

In his book, Bruce R. McConkie makes the following statement about the Holy Ghost:

"In this dispensation, at least, nothing has been revealed as to his origin or destiny; expressions on these matters are both speculative and fruitless" (*Mormon Doctrine*, p. 359).

Mormons also teach that sometimes the designation "Holy Ghost" is used to mean the "power" or "gift" of that personage, not the individual or person who is a member of the Godhead. A study of Mormon writings reveals that the idea that the Holy Ghost is only a "power" is more prevalent than the teaching that he is an actual person.

In fact, many Mormons make a distinction between "Holy Ghost" and "Holy Spirit." They will describe the Holy Ghost as a light bulb and the Holy Spirit as the light that comes from that bulb.

Mormons talk a lot about "receiving the gift of the Holy Ghost by the laying on of hands" but they do not believe that the Holy Ghost himself comes and dwells in the person. They teach that the Holy Ghost "may not tarry" on people. This expression merely indicates that a person is supposed to receive some kind of power from God.

They also teach that the Holy Ghost "is not in any way essential to salvation." This statement reveals that they do not think very much of the Holy Ghost.

. . .

13. KINGDOM OF GOD—Mormons teach that there are three different stages of the "kingdom of God."

a. The Church of Jesus Christ of Latter-day Saints of today is the "kingdom of God on earth." In other words, the LDS Church and the kingdom are one and the same. Mormons believe that when "the LDS Church speaks, God speaks." They believe that the words of the president of the LDS Church are just as binding as their written works. In its early days the LDS Church taught that the government of the U.S.A., and ultimately of the world, would be given to it to administer as God's deputy. When Utah obtained statehood, this teaching had to be played down, even though the idea is still alive among some Mormons.

b. The LDS Church believes that during the millennium the "kingdom of God" will continue on earth, and that it will be both an "ecclesiastical" and a "political" kingdom. It declares that at this time the LDS Church will be in charge of all government as well as all religious affairs.

c. Finally, they teach that in the eternal worlds yet to come, "the celestial kingdom is the kingdom of God."

. . .

14. MAN—Mormonism exalts man. It teaches that man is the "embryo" of a god. The potential to become a god is in every person and, if given the opportunity, will come out. It maintains that this "embryo" can only grow and develop in the womb of the LDS Church. It asserts it has *the truth,* so only those believing in LDS teachings can become a god. It does not believe that man is basically sinful. It teaches that man is basically good, and that this goodness will emerge through being obedient to the teachings of the LDS Church.

Mormons teach that "man and God are of the same race," and man is as divine as Christ himself. They say that we were all spirit-born children of God, that Christ just happened to be the

first child born in the preexistent world. The only difference between Christ and other men, in Mormon doctrine, is that Jesus
was literally begotten of the Father (God) and Mary in this world.
They teach we are spirit brothers of Christ in the full sense of the
word.

· · ·

15. MORTAL AND IMMORTAL BODIES—Mormons
teach that in this life we have mortal bodies, but in the next life
those who enter the celestial kingdom will have immortal bodies. These will be real bodies and, as far as I can discern, will
function the same way our bodies function now. There will be
marriage, family life, progression, etc. These are not the same as
the glorified bodies of which the Bible speaks—bodies like the
resurrected Lord Jesus Christ's body.

· · ·

16. PRIESTHOOD—Mormons speak of two priesthoods—
the Aaronic and the Melchizedek. Most Mormon boys at age
twelve are ordained to the Aaronic priesthood (known as the lesser
priesthood) with the title of "deacon." At the age of nineteen,
these boys are ordained to the Melchizedek priesthood (known
as the greater priesthood) with the title of "elder."

The LDS Church maintains that the priesthood holds the
power and authority of God, and that this has been delegated to
man on earth, to act in all things for the salvation of men. This
practice tends to promote a spirit of superiority and pride among
those who hold these priesthoods.

· · ·

17. REDEMPTION—Mormon doctrine teaches that men
are not responsible for the sins inherited from Adam. The penalty for Adam's sin was physical death. Christ died "uncondition-
ally" for all the sins of Adam. So all humans will be resurrected
and given a body again. "This gift is forced upon mankind which
they cannot reject, though they were disposed." When the Mor-

mons use the word "redemption," they mean that all men will be resurrected.

• • •

18. SCRIPTURE—Mormons claim that any written or spoken message that comes from God to man by the power of the Holy Ghost is "scripture." If it is written and accepted by the LDS Church, it becomes part of the "scriptures" or "standard works." The standard works accepted by the LDS Church are *The Book of Mormon, Doctrine and Covenants,* and *The Pearl of Great Price.* They claim to believe the Bible, but don't list it as a standard work because they say that they believe only those parts that are "translated correctly." They believe that very little of the Bible is translated correctly. They use those parts of the Bible that seem to prove their doctrine but consider those parts that are in conflict with their beliefs to be translated incorrectly.

Joseph Smith produced his own Bible known as the "Inspired Version." He claims he was commanded by God to translate the Bible and have it printed. (Actually it is an "edition" by Joseph Smith and not a translation. Ninety percent of it is the same as the King James Version.) Neither Joseph Smith nor the LDS Church of Salt Lake City obeyed this command to have it printed. They never printed it, but the Reorganized Church of Jesus Christ of Latter-day Saints (which has recently changed its name to the Community of Christ) of Independence, Missouri, published it in 1867. The LDS Church of Salt Lake City does not use the whole of this version because it conflicts too much with their doctrines, but they do quote from certain parts of the ten percent Joseph Smith changed.

Even though the Mormons put a lot of emphasis on *The Book of Mormon,* none of their major doctrines can be found in it. In fact, most of its teaching is in conflict with Mormon doctrine.

The Book of Mormon tells the story of a Jewish family that left Jerusalem in 600 B.C. and came to the Americas. The account starts with Lehi and his wife Sarah (descendants of the tribe of Joseph through Manasseh), and their four sons, Laman, Lemuel, Sam, and Nephi. Lehi is warned in a dream of the coming destruction of Jerusalem which came with the Babylonian captivity. Lehi and his family flee into the wilderness. Nephi is the most spiritual and his brothers rebel against his leadership. The brothers are confounded and Nephi takes the leadership. In two years, eight workers build a ship and then cross the Indian and Pacific Oceans. They land on the narrow piece of land that is Central America. They began to build a civilization in the new world, but there was constant fighting between the Nephites and the Lamanites, the two main groups of people. The Nephites are the "good guys" and the Lamanites are the "bad guys." The skin of the Lamanites turned dark because of their sin. There were times when the Nephites were good people but they fell into sin and needed to repent. There are also times when the "wicked" Lamanites repent, but their skin did not turn light again after repentance. A good part of *The Book of Mormon* deals with various wars.

The Book of Mormon ends in 421 A.D. In 385, the Lamanites engage the Nephites (upon their request) in a final battle at the Hill Cumorah. In this battle, at least 230,000 Nephites were annihilated and only one man, Moroni, the son of Mormon, was left. He then completed the records found in *The Book of Mormon*. After this battle, the Lamanites returned to their native land which was, according to Mormon teaching, in South America.

Many of the characters in *The Book of Mormon* are taken from the Bible with their names and a few of the circumstances changed. Most of the religious material found in *The Book of Mormon* is also taken from the Bible. It has both Old and New Testament teachings, along with some of the false religious ideas of the day in which Joseph Smith lived, all mixed together. Because Smith's purpose in writing *The Book of Mormon* was to make money and not to found a new religion, Mormon doctrine is not contained in it. The Mormons use *The Book of Mormon* only to get people away from the teachings of the Bible and over to the false teachings of Joseph Smith and his successors.

There are many contradictions in the Mormon writings and in the teachings of their presidents. Until recently, whenever a contradiction came to light the Mormon leaders tried to cover it up by saying that the enemies of the Mormon church misquoted what was written or spoken. However, they now teach that the word of the current president of the LDS Church takes precedence over anything that has been previously written or spoken by Joseph Smith or any other past leader, even if it is in conflict with what was written or spoken.

· · ·

19. SIN—As with most false religions, Mormons do not emphasize personal sin. They teach that little children cannot sin and that man's nature is not basically sinful. They say that we are all "gods in embryo." They believe that sin cannot be committed unless laws are ordained and the people have a knowledge of those laws when they violate them. Until a person has a knowledge of these laws, sin is considered to be just a "blunder." To the Mormon, sin is being disobedient to the laws and ordinances of the LDS Church.

· · ·

20. SUPERIORITY—Mormons teach that everyone had a chance to do good works in the preexistent state of probation. They teach that man is born into this world on the merits of the kind of spirit he or she was in the preexistence. Those who were the best in the spirit world are born as white Mormons. They teach that the "saints [Mormons] are the best people." The skin color gets darker as you progress toward those who did the fewest good works. They say the blacks were the least valiant in the spirit world; they narrowly escaped going with Satan and are

cursed by their blackness. (Since 1978 this teaching has been played down.)

Mormons greatly emphasize intelligence, because they believe that this is the means by which a person can be exalted. Even though they will deny it, the Mormons teach that they are of superior intelligence to all other people.

• • •

21. TRINITY—Mormons say they believe in "a" trinity. They do not mean one God in three persons. They believe that there are three gods—the Father, the Son, and the Holy Ghost—with whom we have to do in this universe. They call the Godhead "a" trinity, not "the" Trinity.

What exactly does the Bible teach?

The Bible does not use the word "trinity," but the concept is taught from Genesis to Revelation.

First: the Bible clearly teaches that there is only one God (Deuteronomy 6:4; Isaiah 43:10; 44:6, 8; 45:21–22; 46:9).

Second: the Bible recognizes the Father as God (John 6:27; 5:17–23; Galatians 1:1–3; Ephesians 1:2; 1 Thessalonians 1:1).

Third: the Bible recognizes the Son as God (Matthew 1:23— "Immanuel—God with us"; John 1:4, 14—"The Word was God"; Titus 2:13; Hebrews 1:8; etc.).

Fourth: the Bible recognizes the Holy Spirit as God (Acts 5:3–4—Lying to the Holy Spirit is lying to God; etc.).

WITHIN THE NATURE OF THE ONE TRUE GOD
THERE ETERNALLY EXIST THREE DISTINCT PERSONS,*
GOD THE FATHER, GOD THE SON, AND GOD THE HOLY SPIRIT.
THESE THREE ARE ONE GOD, THE SAME IN SUBSTANCE,*
EQUAL IN POWER AND GLORY.

* Person: A more technical and philosophical term is "hypostasis," meaning "distinct subsistence." Theologians ordinarily use the word "persons," not because it is adequate, but because the Bible speaks of the relationship of the three in a manner similar to what exists between human persons. God is not

. . .

22. THE TRUE CHURCH—Mormons emphasize that The Church of Jesus Christ of Latter-day Saints is the only true and living church upon the face of the earth. They claim it is the only organization authorized to preach the gospel and administer the ordinances of salvation—which is a long process. It claims it is the only church which has the power to save and exalt men in the hereafter. They say, "Membership in this divine institution is a pearl of great price."

---

lonely, but has a fullness of life and fellowship in Himself. But theologians do not mean, by using the words "persons" and "substance," that God is physical.

Chapter Five

How the Mormon Church Is Organized

THE Mormon church was organized on April 6, 1830, at the home of Peter Whitmer Sr., in Fayette, Seneca County, New York. The official name now is "The Church of Jesus Christ of Latter-day Saints."

LDS governmental structure is quite different from that of other religious groups. Church offices are grouped under two priesthoods: the most important of these is the Melchizedek priesthood; the lesser is known as the Aaronic priesthood.

Melchizedek Priesthood

A. THE FIRST PRESIDENCY. The President of the church has two counselors: the First Counselor and the Second Counselor. These three together constitute the First Presidency, and they "preside over and direct all the affairs of the kingdom."

B. THE TWELVE APOSTLES (THE COUNCIL OF THE TWELVE). Their duties are "to build up the Church and regulate all the affairs of the same, in all nations, under the direction of the First Presidency of the Church."

C. ASSISTANTS TO THE COUNCIL OF THE TWELVE. At present there are 21 men in this group.

D. THE COUNCIL OF THE SEVENTY. There are seven presidents over the 70 (i.e., one over every ten) and one of the seven presidents is president over them.

E. PRESIDING BISHOPRIC. This body consists of men who administer the temporal affairs of the Church under the direction of the First Presidency. They have jurisdiction over the Church's local bishops.

F. THE PATRIARCH OF THE CHURCH. The calling of a patriarch is to bless the members of the Church. This office is a hereditary one. Joseph Smith's father held this office and it goes to the oldest man of the bloodline of Joseph Smith.

G. ELDER. An elder can be appointed at the early age of 19. He has authority to baptize and to lay on hands for the gift of the Holy Spirit. Elder is a very common title—all male missionaries are known as "elders." They are to administer in spiritual things.

Aaronic Priesthood

A. BISHOP. Each ward (congregation) is governed by a bishop and two counselors. The bishop's duty is to administer in all temporal things. He is supposed to be a literal descendant of Aaron. (Since this is not possible, the way they get around it is by saying that when a person becomes a Mormon his Gentile blood is taken out and he is given Jewish blood.)

B. PRIEST. A young man is ordained a priest at the age of 16.

C. TEACHER. A boy is ordained a teacher at the age of 14.

D. DEACON. A boy is ordained a deacon at the age of 12. Deacons are allowed to serve communion, which, by the way, is bread and water.

Chapter Six

Mormon Business Connections

FROM time to time you may have heard rumors that the Mormon church owns various businesses, but it is difficult to come up with any conclusive evidence. I heard a number of these rumors and decided to give the Mormon church an opportunity to answer for itself. At the time, I was corresponding with the man who was third in line to be president of the Mormon church. I wrote to him and mentioned the name of a supermarket chain that I had heard belonged to the LDS Church. I asked him if this was true, and also asked him to give me a list of the companies owned by the Church so that in the future I could give out correct information. In his reply, he laughed at the idea that they owned the company I had named and would not give a definite answer. He said that they did own some welfare farms and other sites, but would not tell me the names of any of these concerns. He tried to make me think that they were not involved in any for-profit enterprise. At the time, I did not have any concrete evidence and could not dispute what he said. However, after I obtained the facts about their businesses, I corresponded with another Mormon official and was able to refute what he said because of substantial information I had already obtained about their business connections. Having this information could prove to be helpful in witnessing to Mormons.

The Mormon church has been quite successful in keeping its financial empire a secret, particularly from those outside the state of Utah. The latest figures of assets that I have been able to obtain for the Church's holdings, including its vast business enterprise, would seem to be a minimum of $30 billion. It has been estimated that its annual income is $5.9 billion. The Church does not publish any reports about its direct income nor about its businesses and the income received from them. Two Associated Press reporters conducted an extensive investigation of Mormon businesses. When the truth about their businesses became public, the Mormons said that the purpose of these businesses was to help finance their religious activities along with their welfare system. However, evidence shows that the Church's charities receive relatively little money from its corporations.

The president of the Mormon church is Chairman of the Board for many of these corporations. The 12 apostles and other Church officials are figurehead members of the boards. They receive salaries for these positions even though they are affiliated in name only, since they do not spend much time in board meetings. The Mormons continually mention that their officials serve the Church without salaries. They never mention the fact that they are paid a "living allowance" (I don't know what the difference is) and also that they receive salaries from these corporations because they are Mormon officials.

Some of the businesses that are run or controlled by the Mormon church include:

• The Utah-Idaho, Inc. (formerly called Utah-Idaho Sugar Co.), in which the Church holds approximately a 50 percent controlling interest. This firm has controlling interest in Gourmet Food Products, Inc., Boardman, Oregon, and also has irrigated farmland in southeastern Idaho and southern Washington.

• Five ZCMI department stores.

• The Acme supermarket chain.

• Three insurance companies: Beneficial Life Insurance Co.,

Utah Home Fire and Insurance Co., and Deseret Mutual Benefit Association.

• The newspaper *Deseret News,* with interest in the Salt Lake *Tribune*.

• Television stations KSL in Salt Lake City and KIRO in Seattle. It also owns 11 radio stations in Salt Lake City, New York, Los Angeles, Seattle, Kansas City, Chicago and San Francisco. These are owned under the name of the Bonneville International Corp., which also has other media-related interests.

• Deseret Books, which has seven stores in Utah and Southern California.

• Deseret Press, which prints magazines, paperback books, and hardback books.

• The Utah Hotel Co., which owns the 406-room Hotel Utah, the 186-room Temple Square Hotel and the 160-room Utah Motor Lodge.

• Beehive Clothing Mills, with plants in Utah, England, and Mexico that manufacture temple clothing and garments worn only by church faithfuls.

• A 312,000-acre Deseret Cattle and Citrus Ranch near Disney World, Florida. This is the top beef ranch in the world. It is estimated to be worth $858,000,000 and is entirely owned by the LDS Church.

• A 36-story apartment building in New York City.

• The ZCMI Center in Salt Lake City is a mall which includes the 20-story Beneficial Life office tower.

• A computer firm.

• Deseret Trust Co.

• AgReseves, the largest producer of nuts in America.

• Bonneville International Corp.

• Dozens of commercial buildings in Salt Lake City, including the Kennecott, Union Pacific, J.C.Penny's, Utah Power & Light, Constitution, Medical Arts and Beneficial Life buildings and a 10-story parking garage.

• Church insurance companies hold stock in numerous utilities, railroads, and other corporations, all listed with the Utah Insurance Commissioner. The Church has acknowledged ownership of stock in the Times-Mirror Corp. which publishes the *Los Angeles Times* and has other holdings.

From this list, you can see how much power the Mormon church has in Utah and in business circles because of its vast financial empire.

Chapter Seven

Mormon Morals

THE LDS Church has spent millions of dollars in a great effort to present a good image of itself to the general public. In most cases, this seems to have been successful. When talking to the average person about Mormons, you will find that he thinks of them as clean-living, hard-working people. The clean-cut, nicely dressed Mormon missionaries, along with the Mormon Tabernacle Choir (singing hymns containing truths they do not believe), has helped to strengthen this image. The literature they prepare for distribution to non-Mormons is written so that the non-Christian doctrines of the LDS Church—which is *most* of their doctrines—do not offend, because they use the Bible to seemingly prove them. In fact, they claim to be "more Biblical" than any other Christian group. If their literature is taken at face value, they seem to come close to true Christianity. This is part of their plan for deceiving the public. Often when one first meets a Mormon and asks about certain of their non-Biblical doctrines, the Mormon will be very evasive and may even deny their teachings. For this reason it is important to know what Mormons *really* believe, so that you will not be misled but be able to help them to face up to their beliefs.

Several year ago the Mormon church ran a series of four ads (at a cost of over two million dollars) in the *Reader's Digest*. They were well-written ads and were part of their campaign to deceive the public. These ads were full of bold falsehoods and misleading statements.

For a long time I had accepted, to a degree, this propaganda—until I started to investigate their claims. I did not think that a religious group would tell outright lies about their religion, but I was mistaken.

I began my investigation after talking to a well-informed friend about Mormonism. He happened to mention that there are at least 20,000 known cases of polygamy in Utah today. I asked him why the state officials did not do something about it. His reply was startling. He stated that since Utah presently spends so much money on social welfare, they did not wish to add another 20,000 people to this already-heavy burden. This was exactly the opposite of what I had heard regarding the Mormons' welfare system: it was supposed to be so excellent that very few members ever needed to turn to the state for help. I recalled an article in the *Los Angeles Times* about the Mormon welfare system that had been reprinted in the *Japan Times* a few years back. The opening statement was: "Almost no Mormons are on public welfare"—truly a bold claim!

In the Mormons' paid advertisement in the *Reader's Digest*, they made the following assertion:

> To accept government handouts in money or food, they believe, may sacrifice self-respect and independence. . . . In these times of ever-mounting dole and welfare bills, the self-reliance of Mormons makes them stand out—as families, as Americans.

I therefore wrote to the Library of Congress for information about public welfare. The information I received was revealing. I discovered there are a number of states that have a much lower welfare expenditure, per capita, than Utah. Utah, with a 70% Mormon population, should have the lowest welfare expenditures in

America if its claims are true, but the evidence proves otherwise.

The Mormons run a number of "welfare" farms. A while back the state of California investigated a so-called "welfare orange grove" run by the Mormon church and found that 85% of the oranges were sold for profit on the open market. Only 5% of the oranges were utilized for welfare. The remaining 10% went elsewhere. Upon investigation, California revoked its tax exempt status because the orange grove was a profit-making business. A similar case occurred in Idaho, where the Mormons have a cattle ranch. Upon investigation there, the state found that it too was a profit-making business.

Many of the Mormon meeting places (known as "wards") have their own gardens in which they grow vegetables for "welfare purposes." The Mormons give their time "free" to help grow the vegetables. Even though it costs the Mormon church nothing, the people who receive these welfare benefits are expected to pay for the help they receive. In most cases, any help that the Mormons give must be reimbursed. How can this be classified as welfare?

A Mormon told me that the Mormon divorce rate was only about 2%. I checked and found that he was way off. Utah, with a 70% Mormon population, has a divorce rate which is right up with the national average—but high for *that* part of the nation.

Many of these divorces have actually been encouraged by the Mormon church. Some couples break up because one party either refuses to become a Mormon or else is leaving the Church, especially if the reason for leaving is "apostasy" (becoming a born-again Christian).

The Mormons also claim that they have very little problem with crime. However, when I checked the crime rate for Utah I found it was right up with the national average. Salt Lake City, which is 50% Mormon, has a surprisingly high crime rate.

Mormons continually refer to themselves as "moral" people.

In their advertisement in the *Reader's Digest*, they made the following claim:

> HOME IS THE ROCK. Today, the threats to the American family and home are far different, but no less real: permissiveness and promiscuity, divorce and drugs, breakdown of parental authority, lack of communication between parents and children. But in the face of these, most Mormon homes, because of their religious convictions, are as secure now as they were in pioneer days.

Once again, upon investigating I found out that the Mormons have a real problem with teenage pregnancies. And along with their high rate of sexual immorality, Utah has many cases of venereal disease. Drugs are also a serious problem among them.

In their visitation efforts and on the radio, Mormons talk about their Monday-evening family night called "Family Home Evening." They urge people to get together as a family for at least half an hour of fun. Because of this program, many people get the idea that Mormons have a good family life. However, when one takes a close look at the average Mormon family, the opposite becomes obvious. The father is gone most nights of the week on church business, and the mother has several days and some nights that she has to be active in the church organizations. Ask the children of many a "good" Mormon family and you will find that outside of the Monday night activities they have very little family life.

The Mormons have about 60,000 missionaries around the world going from door to door or talking to people on the streets seven days a week. (They have one day a week off, and then only until five in the afternoon.) Yet if Christians go to visit Mormon homes, the Mormons readily become indignant and ask why we are bothering them. Sometimes they become obnoxious.

When the missionaries first come to visit you, they will seem "polite as Polly." If you begin to witness to them with some knowledge, they can become rude to you—in your own home. I have had some use very unbecoming language.

Mormons are well-trained in character assassination. When they do not know what to say, they will question the motives and character of the one to whom they are talking. You can tell when a Mormon is defeated because he will cunningly start attacking your character and motives. One of their favorite phrases is, "I thought you were really sincere, but now I see that you are not."

How paradoxical! Mormons will stoop to question the sincerity of others, yet they will ignore a mountain of evidence—in records and historical documents locked up in their archives—that proves their religion to be fraudulent. It seems that if the Mormons were sincere and desirous of truth, they would make these records available to the public. As you may expect, these documents are extremely hard to gain access to, for their contents prove that Mormonism is false.

Through repeated contact with numerous Mormons, I have found that telling the truth is not one of their virtues. Lying is quite commonly practiced. Not only do the missionaries lie, but also the officials who run the Mormon church. I have in my file two letters from Mormon officials that contain falsehoods. One man was so bold as to suggest that I should check his answer, if I wished. I did, and found that he was not being truthful.

The Mormon church runs a highly sophisticated and vast "intelligence agency." At their 28-story headquarters building in Salt Lake City, the top two floors are given over entirely to this purpose. No one can obtain access to these two floors without special permission.

As I write this chapter, I have been reminded of the severe condemnation that Jesus laid upon the Pharisees—words which would apply equally to the Mormons. Matthew 23:15 says: "Woe unto you, scribes and Pharisees, hypocrites! For ye compass sea and land to make one proselyte, and when he is made, ye make him twofold more the child of hell than yourselves."

An appropriate warning concerning the Mormons is found in Matthew 7:15: "Beware of false prophets, who come to you in sheep's clothing, but inwardly they are ravening wolves."

And yet, though "evil men and seducers shall wax worse and worse, deceiving and being deceived"—as Paul cautioned Timothy about false teachers to come—let us neither fear nor despair. For "all scripture is given by inspiration of God, and is profitable for reproof, for correction, for instruction in righteousness" (2 Timothy 3:16). Let us believe His Word. Our God can open spiritually blinded eyes and most marvelously correct and transform the deluded!

Those two young men who stand at your door are candidates for the Savior's "extreme makeover"—if you are faithful to seize the opportunity!

Chapter Eight

Beginning the Conversation

IF you wish to be an effective Christian witness, begin your conversation with the Mormon missionaries by asking about their family, their home state, sports, hobbies, etc.—and remember what they said. (I usually take notes to help me remember.) If the weather is hot, offer your visitors a glass of cold water. (Note: Do not offer tea, coffee or Coke, because they do not drink such beverages, at least where people can see them.) Then say something like this: "Before we start talking about religion in detail, let's get to know each other better. If you will each tell me 'why' you became a Mormon, I will tell you why I came to believe as I do." (At this point don't tell them you are a Christian. They have a stereotyped impression about Christians and will categorize you as such and not really listen to you. But if they don't know where you are coming from, they will listen better. I usually have them sitting on the edge of the chair when I give my testimony.) "That way our time together should be more profitable."

Give them each a chance first to tell you "why" he became a Mormon. In most cases at least one will say something like: "I was brought up in a Mormon family and was baptized into the Mormon church at the age of 8. When I was 17 years old [usually, but sometimes a few years before or after] I prayed about

Mormonism [or *The Book of Mormon*] to see if it was the true religion. I received a 'burning in the bosom' which confirmed to me that the Mormon church is the true church."

When they have finished, give *your* testimony as to how you came to know Jesus Christ as your personal Savior. When I do this, I usually take about 20 to 30 minutes to give my testimony in full detail.

Here, briefly, is my testimony.

I was born in Clearfield, in the central part of Pennsylvania. My parents were not Christians then, but my father always took us to Sunday School. Once I asked my mother a question about the Bible. She couldn't answer me, so I felt I couldn't get much help from my parents.

One night when I was six years old, as I lay in my bed I thought, "What would happen if I died in my sleep?" I didn't know anything about the way of salvation at the time. I felt that I needed some special preparation to get into heaven, but I didn't know what. In order not to die in my sleep, I decided not to go to sleep. Of course, eventually I did fall asleep.

The same question came to me every night for a week. Though I was only six, it was very real to me. From that time on, I realized I was carrying a heavy burden. Every time I sinned, it became heavier. As my years in grade school progressed, the burden on my heart became even heavier. I wanted to get rid of this burden, but didn't know how.

Some people said, "Just do the best you can, and since God is 'a God of love,' everything will be okay." This didn't satisfy me. If the way to get to heaven was to do more good things than bad, it didn't give me much hope. It seemed I naturally always did more bad deeds than good ones.

Once I entered junior high school, I not only was carrying this heavy burden of sin but I could not see any reason for living. After all, why was man put on earth? I was not satisfied with my life and had few examples of people who were.

In the summer of 1942 we moved to Chester, Pennsylvania,

where my father got a job working in the shipyard during World War II. The pastor of a small community church came visiting one August afternoon shortly after we moved in and invited our family to church. My father, four brothers, my sister and I went the next Sunday. We almost doubled the attendance of the Sunday School. This was a gospel-preaching church where people diligently studied the Bible. I enjoyed going to Sunday School and soon became active in the young people's group.

The next year in October there was a city-wide evangelistic campaign in our town. The Saturday night before it began, our young people's group went downtown and gave out invitations to the meeting. I went to the meeting Tuesday night and about 3000 people showed up. I felt good, thinking that maybe some people were there because I had given out invitations.

The evangelist began to speak on sin, but in a different way than I had ever heard it before. He did not talk about war, drunkards, thieves, etc., but said that pride, self-centeredness, selfishness, anger, wrath, lying, cheating, gossiping, jealousy, covetousness, backbiting, disobedience to parents, fighting with brothers and sisters, etc., were awful sins before God. He didn't say we were just tainted with sin, but that we were all ungodly, wicked sinners before God. This did not go down too well with me. I was considered a "good boy" in our area because my father was a strict disciplinarian, for which I am thankful. I knew I was not perfect, but to be called a wicked, ungodly sinner made me so angry I didn't hear anything else the evangelist said.

As I left the meeting that night, I determined that I would not go back to any more meetings that week. I wanted to forget everything that rude evangelist had said. But God had other plans.

As I went to bed that Tuesday night I recalled thirteen actual sins. I wasn't proud of this, but I also didn't think thirteen sins for a fourteen-year-old boy was too bad. Wednesday night as I went to bed, the Holy Spirit brought to mind some more sins. My list grew from thirteen to twenty-five. Thursday night I began counting at twenty-six and got up to fifty. That night I thought, "Maybe that evangelist was right about my sins and I was wrong." Well, Friday night I settled the issue. I continued counting from fifty-one and got up to one hundred. Then my whole past life exploded—and many more sins came pouring in upon me. These were not just general sin categories but actual sins. For the first time in my life, I realized what a sinner I was before the holy and righteous God of the Bible! It was very humbling.

Fortunately, the next night I found the answer to my sins. Twice a month on Saturday night many young people from various churches in our city got together for a meeting. I went and was glad I did! The speaker's message was on sin, but this time I could not argue with him because God had revealed part of my sinful heart to me. "The Bible tells us," he said, "that Jesus Christ came into this world to save sinners. If we will acknowledge our sins and believe that Jesus Christ died on the cross for us, then we can be saved."

As I sat there, I said to myself, "Am I really hearing what this man is saying? He said I am an ungodly sinner. I know that's true. He also said Jesus Christ died for sinners. Since I am a sinner, then I qualify for the salvation that Jesus Christ is offering."

Right there I bowed my head, confessed my sins, and asked Jesus to come into my life and save me from my sins. At that very moment I felt the burden of my sins lifted. For the first time in my life I was free. Then I realized what was missing in my life. God created me to have fellowship with Himself, but sin had come in and separated me from God. I hadn't known the reason I had been created. That's why I lacked any purpose for living. When God took away my sins, He brought me into a living fellowship with Himself. I left the meeting that night with a light heart and a reason for living.

The next day, Sunday, as I went to church, it had a new and deep meaning for me. I will never forget when they talked about God being our Father—because now I knew Him in a personal way. Monday, as I entered school, I realized I was a different person and that God was going with me.

Having been taught that when you know Christ as your Savior you are to read your Bible and pray every day, this I began to do. What I read in the Bible surprised me because it was such a personal book. It was as if it were written just for me. I didn't realize then how God knew my heart so well. Of course the Word of God began to convict me of any sins I committed and had a cleansing effect on my life.

In this way, very quietly, without arguing or having interruptions, I have been able to present the complete plan of salvation in my testimony and explain the way to heaven, which was my goal.

Your personal testimony will obviously be different from mine—perhaps more dramatic, or maybe less. Whatever the case, make it explicit. In presenting the plan of salvation, do not use vague terms, but explain very simply what you mean. The following examples will help you in giving your testimony clearly:

• • •

1. SIN—Mormons have no true concept of sin. They believe that children cannot sin until the age of eight. They also believe that man is not basically sinful. When you use the word "sin," explain exactly what the Bible says about it. Instead of saying, "I realized that I was a sinner," say, "I realized my heart was filled with pride, selfishness, self-centeredness, self-righteousness, envy, conceit, strife, evil speaking, covetousness, boasting, etc." Explain that fighting with brothers and sisters and being disobedient to parents is also sin in the sight of God. Name these sins very slowly and tell of actual times when you were envious or angry. Do not talk at length about drinking, smoking, adultery, because Mormons also speak out against these sins. Emphasize inward sins, of which we all are guilty.

• • •

2. BORN AGAIN—This term has no specific meaning to a Mormon like it does to an evangelical Christian. In fact, if you ask a Mormon if he has been "born again," often he will answer "Yes." If you were to ask him what "born again" means, after he said "Yes," he could not give you a very clear answer. (To Mormons, being born again is a lengthy process which never can be

completed during this earthly life.) He only says "Yes" to deceive you into thinking that he doesn't believe very differently from you, when in reality this is not at all true. His faith does not resemble the true Christian faith at all. So it is best not to use this term with a Mormon. If you want to use the term "born from above," that would be much better and save a lot of confusion.

• • •

3. HEAVEN—Mormons believe that almost everyone goes to heaven, so the fact that you have the assurance of going to heaven when you die means nothing to them. They believe in three heavens, with a different class of people going to each one.

a. THE CELESTIAL KINGDOM is only for good Mormons. However, none of them has the assurance of going there, not even the president of the Mormon church.

b. THE TERRESTRIAL KINGDOM is for honorable people who in this life did not accept the LDS teachings.

c. THE TELESTIAL KINGDOM is for all the wicked people of the world.

It is best to talk about having assurance of going to the celestial kingdom, or going to be with God the Father when you die, so that they will understand what you are talking about.

• • •

4. THE DEITY OF CHRIST—Mormons teach that Christ is "a god" and not "the God." They also teach that there is "a" Trinity, which means there are three gods (God the Father, God the Son, and God the Holy Spirit), but they deny "the" Trinity (i.e., one God in three persons). Therefore, you need to make it clear that you believe in one God manifested in three persons. (I will elaborate much more on this later.)

• • •

5. SALVATION—Mormons believe that you can merit salvation by your own efforts. Most people like this kind of religion, because it inflates their pride—"Look at all the good things

I am doing." It is humbling to have to admit that we are ungodly sinners before the holy and righteous God, and that there is nothing that we can do to earn or merit our salvation. This is very difficult for humans because of our pride.

Because Mormons believe that salvation is a matter of their own effort by observing a long list of "do's and don'ts," it is best not to say that all one has to do is just "believe in Jesus" to be saved. While this is true, it comes across entirely different to a Mormon. He will interpret this to mean that all you have to do is say you are sorry to God for the wrong things you have done, and then you can go out and live any way you want to and still get to heaven. Actually, the Biblical way of salvation is the most difficult way there is. Who *wants* to admit to being such an ungodly, wicked sinner that only God Almighty can solve his problem of sin! This truth makes me very, very sinful—and is very humbling.

For this reason, when I am witnessing to Mormons I will say, "The Biblical way of salvation is very hard and just too difficult for you to ever enter into." The one I am talking to will usually ask, "Why is it too hard for me to enter into?" I will reply, "There is no use explaining it to you because I know it is too difficult for you." He will ask the second time, "Why is it too difficult?" Again I say, "It is just too difficult, so there is no use even explaining it to you." Again he will inquire as to why it is too difficult. Then I will say, "Since you insist on knowing, I will tell you why. In 1 Timothy 1:15 the Apostle Paul said that he was 'the chief of sinners.'" I then inquire, "Will you right now make the same confession as Paul, that you too are the chief of sinners?" Every time I have asked this question the answer has been "No." Then I say, "See, I told you so. In order to be saved the *Biblical way* you must admit the awful sinfulness of your heart. Only as one is willing to admit his sinfulness and is willing to confess it to God and ask for the salvation provided by the blood of the Lord Jesus Christ that was shed upon the cross, can one really be born into the family of God."

A Few Fundamental Questions: Sin

When you have finished giving your testimony, question your listeners concerning what they said when you asked "why" they became a Mormon. Mormons teach that in order to join the LDS Church a person needs faith, repentance, baptism by immersion, and the possibility of receiving the Holy Spirit by the laying on of hands. (Actually they know nothing of the Holy Spirit.) Explain to them that you have some questions about their testimony. You might say: "If I understand LDS doctrine correctly, it teaches that you must 'repent' before you can be baptized. I also believe it teaches that children cannot sin before the age of eight. You just said you were baptized when you were eight, but according to LDS teachings you did not have any sins to repent of! How could there have been true repentance if you had not sinned? Why did they let you join the church without true repentance?" (He will probably not be able to give you a good answer.)

This is a very important LDS teaching to understand. Because the Mormons have a faulty view of sin they have a faulty view of salvation. Since they don't believe that they were born in sin or are big sinners, they do not feel they need a big Savior. Until a person understands something of the Biblical view of the awfulness of sin he will not see his need of accepting Jesus Christ exclusively, without works, to be his own personal Savior.

References in LDS writings that teach that children are born pure and innocent and can't be tempted or sin until the age of eight are found in a number of LDS writings. In *The Book of Mormon*, in Moroni 8:8 (on page 525) it states:

> Listen to the words of Christ, your Redeemer, your Lord and your God. Behold, I came into the world not to call the righteous

but sinners to repentance; the whole need no physician, but they that are sick; wherefore, little children are whole, for they are *not capable of committing sin*; wherefore the curse of Adam is taken from them in me, that it hath no power over them; and the law of circumcision is done away in me. [Emphases added.]

And the book *Doctrine and Covenants*, Section 29:46–47, states on page 46:

But behold, I say unto you, that little children are redeemed from the foundation of the world through mine Only Begotten; wherefore, *they cannot sin*, for power is not given unto Satan to tempt little children, until they begin to become accountable before me. [Emphases added.]

The LDS Church teaches that at the age of eight one reaches the "age of accountability." In *The Book of Mormon*, Moroni 8:11, page 525, we read:

And their little children need no repentance, neither baptism.

Then in *Doctrine and Covenants*, Section 68, verse 27 (on page 112) we read:

And their children shall be baptized for the remission of their sins when eight years old, and receive the laying on of the hands.

In the book *Doctrines of Salvation*, Vol. II, written by Joseph Fielding Smith (a previous president of the LDS Church), it states on page 49:

SALVATION OF CHILDREN. False Doctrine of Guilt For Original Sin. There are millions of people, professing to believe in Christ, who believe that little children are under condemnation and tainted with original sin—which is as *damnable* a doctrine as was ever taught among the children of men, for *little children are not tainted with sin*. . . . the Lord has not placed *any* taint upon little children who come into this world. . . . Every spirit of man was innocent in the beginning. [Emphasis in the text.]

And in the same book, on page 53, we find:

How could you teach a little child to repent? It has not anything to repent of.

Remember, one is considered a child until the age of eight, and only *after* that is he capable of sinning. If he does something wrong it is merely a mistake, and he is not accountable. So before this, repentance is not necessary or possible.

Therefore, despite what you have said, when the Mormon is pressed for an answer he is likely to say that "sin is not sin until you know it is sin." For the LDS Church claims that the bad things children do is in *ignorance* and not really "sin." But let us be logical: If children are not born in sin, *cannot* be tempted by Satan, and *cannot* sin until the age of eight, how are we to account for some universally acknowledged experiences of childhood?

To show the fallacy in this LDS doctrine, ask the one you are talking to if he ever fought with his brothers or sisters before the age of eight? Wait for an answer. If he is honest, he will have to answer "Yes." You can reply, "You mean that your mother or father never taught you that it was wrong to fight with your brothers or sisters until the age of eight!" Ask him if he ever disobeyed his parents before the age of eight. Again, if he is truthful he will have to say "Yes." Ask him if he doesn't think disobeying his parent is a sin. (Wait for an answer.) Ask him if his mother and father never told him, before he reached the age of eight, that it was wrong to disobey them! This ought to show him that he *did* sin before the age of eight and it was *not* done in ignorance, so he is *accountable* for it—which is contrary to Mormon teachings.

Continue questioning him by asking if he ever told a lie, stole a cookie or anything, used any bad words, lost his temper, etc., before the age of eight. I had the privilege in Japan of leading a Mormon missionary to salvation through our Lord Jesus Christ, and one of the things that bothered him as a Mormon was this teaching that you cannot sin until the age of eight—which he already felt was not true.

There is another serious problem that needs to be dealt with if a person maintains that children are born pure and innocent and cannot sin until the age of eight. If children are not *born* with and do not have a sin nature, then sin has to be something that is *taught*. By whom? If a Mormon was raised in Utah, he can't easily put the blame on a fallen, corrupt *culture*—the TV, radio, or newspapers—because most of these outlets are owned by the LDS Church. So here comes the logical question: "How do children learn to sin?" Since parents have the most influence on children and control their upbringing, one has to come to the conclusion that Mormon *parents* have taught their children how to sin. What an indictment! (Take your time and go over these matters very slowly and thoroughly. For a faulty view of sin always leads to a faulty view of God, Jesus Christ, the Holy Spirit and salvation.)

Faith, Repentance and Baptism

You might continue by saying, "I see another serious problem. I believe that the LDS Church teaches that one needs 'faith' before he can become a member of the Mormon church. You told me that you did not know that the Mormon church was the right one until you were_____ [age when he received "the burning in the bosom"]. That says to me that you did not have real faith at the time you joined the church. It seems that what the LDS Church teaches about faith and repentance does not mean very much." (Again, he will not have much to say.)

"I am interested in knowing what one has to believe in order to join the LDS Church." What constitutes the right kind of 'faith'? (Listen well to what he has to say, because he will only tell you a portion of the Church's beliefs and try to deceive you.) Mormons usually say that "faith in Jesus Christ" is absolutely necessary. This might sound good, but the LDS Church's meaning is far different from what the Bible teaches. In the first place, the Jesus he is talking about is not the Jesus of the Bible. The LDS Church teaches that Jesus just happened to be the first spirit born in the spirit world and is no different from all the other spirits; and it teaches that the human Jesus is the "literal" son of God the Father and Mary. (Remember, the god of the Mormons is supposed to have a physical body.) The Church also teaches that Christ died only for the sins that you inherit in Adam and only for the sins that you repent of.

While the LDS Church teaches that faith in Jesus Christ is necessary to exaltation, there are many other things one must also believe that are just as important as belief in Jesus Christ. Part of the list of things that one must believe are: (1) that Joseph Smith was a true prophet of God; (2) that only the LDS Church has "the truth"; (3) that it is guided by a living prophet—the president, who can receive "revelation" from God which is equal to Scripture; (4) that one must be 100% in submission to the LDS Church; (5) that *The Book of Mormon* is inspired of God; (6) that baptism is essential to salvation; (7) that one must continue to have "repentance"; (8) that one must endure to the end; (9) that God has a human body and was once a sinful man who used to live on another planet before becoming a god; (10) that it is possible now for men to advance toward godhood; and (11) that in the end one must stand before God to be judged for the things he did in this life.

I liken their beliefs to building a car. A chassis is essential in order to build a car, but a chassis is not a car. You need an engine, transmission, tires, body, seats, etc. So don't be deceived when a Mormon tells you that Jesus Christ is essential to salvation. He likens Jesus Christ to the chassis. He means that Jesus is only one of the many necessary beliefs of the LDS Church.

I have often asked Mormons to tell me everything that is necessary to be sure of getting to the celestial kingdom. They will say that you have to believe in Jesus—and stop there, if you don't keep questioning them. I then ask if this is *all* you need to do. They will say that you need to be baptized. I then ask them if I believe in Jesus and am baptized, is *that* enough? They will have to say "No" and tell me that I need to be a member of the LDS Church. I continue by asking if these three steps are the only things necessary. Then they will have to add some of the other matters listed above. They do not want to tell you all the requirements until after you become a member of the LDS Church. However, in this way I *force* them to tell me just what they believe. As they go down the list I say, "This really gets complicated. Have you done all of these things and are you 100% sure of going to the celestial kingdom the very moment you die?" Of course, they will have to answer "No."

Continue your conversation by asking, "I understand that the LDS Church teaches that baptism is for the remission of sins, and is an essential step in becoming a member of the Church—all of which *starts* one on the road that has the *possibility* of leading to exaltation (becoming a god). It seems to me that since you did not have real faith until age 17 [or whatever age he mentioned in his testimony], and had not repented before being baptized—since you had no sins to repent of at the age of eight—that your baptism then was not valid. It seems reasonable to me that you obviously need to be baptized *again*, for how can you possibly receive the Holy Spirit and be genuinely sealed [this is their teaching] if your baptism was not *after* you had repented! (Pause and give him time to reflect on this doctrinal puzzle.)

"A Burning in the Bosom"

One more important step in questioning your Mormon instructor is about the "feeling" that he claims he felt when he received assurance that the LDS Church was the true church (or that *The Book of Mormon* is true—whichever one he mentioned when he gave his testimony). His avowal of "a burning in the bosom" was part of his memorized speech. You can use it to your advantage. The following questions zero in on this "burning in the bosom."

Christian: You mentioned a feeling that you received, which gave you the assurance that the Mormon church is the true church. What is this feeling like?

Mormon: It's really hard to describe. You have to experience it to know what it's like.

C: Can't you give me some idea of what kind of feeling it is? After all, you are basing your eternal soul's destiny on this feeling.

M: It's something that can't really be described. You have to experience it yourself.

C: There are many different kinds of feelings. Is it like the feeling you get when you go out on your first date? Is it like the feeling you get if your grade is the best one in your class at school? Is it like the feeling you get when you think you have fallen in love with a girl? Would it be similar to any of these feelings?

M: Well, it's really hard to describe just what this feeling is like.

C: This seems rather confusing to me. This feeling is such an important thing in your life, yet you can't give me any idea of what it is like. However, you said that you got this feeling after you had prayed. Could you tell me something about this process of praying? Do you have to pray one time, two times, or many times? Was this a short prayer or a long prayer?

M: Well, it depends upon the person.

C: You're getting me greatly confused. You said you got "a feeling" by praying, but you can't tell me anything about this "feeling" or how one goes about praying for it. But since you prayed for it, let me ask you about your experience. Did you pray just once, twice, or did you have to pray many times? Were your prayers long or short? Surely you can tell me about *your* experience.

M: (You probably will not get an answer. This talk about a "feeling" is something they have memorized for their presentation. When they are questioned, they cannot tell you anything about it.)

• • •

When dealing with a Mormon or any other cultist it is difficult to come to a conclusion on any one subject and move on to another subject the first time you discuss it. You often have to go back over the same topic a number of times before they understand what you are talking about. I will often drop a subject and then the next week will say, "I have been thinking about what we discussed last week and am not satisfied." This way I can ask them more questions on the subject. I might bring up the same subject over a course of several weeks.

• • •

Sometimes the Mormon missionaries will ask you a few questions in order to start an argument. You need to be prepared for this. The questions that might be asked and the answers to them are these:

Christian Denominations

"What denomination do you belong to?" When I am asked this, I reply: "I belong to the only true church set forth in the Bible." Usually the elder will remark that there are many church groups and again ask which one I belong to. Again I say, "I belong to the only true church. This is the church of which Jesus

Christ is the head, and all born-from-above believers belong to it."

Mormons love to declare that there are 900 (sometimes as many as 1,200) Christian denominations, all of which claim to be the only true church. They say the many groups teach conflicting doctrines, yet base those doctrines on the Bible. The Mormon will ask you, "How can all these denominations be right?" The usual Christian response is to point out: (1) there are not that many groups, and (2) the doctrinal differences among true Christian groups are not as diverse as the Mormons think. This, however, is not an adequate answer. The elders will not be paying attention to your explanation. Nor will they "buy" it. To get their attention, say, "900 denominations are a lot, aren't they?"

Mormon: Yes, they certainly are.

Christian: Let's see. Christianity is 2,000 years old and in that time 900 denominations have developed, according to you. Mormonism is only 170 years old, but there are 83 different groups that point to Joseph Smith as their founder. It seems to me that Mormonism is divided worse than Christianity. (Of these 83 groups, the next six largest are: Reorganized Church of Jesus Christ of Latter-day Saints (which has recently changed its name to "Community of Christ"), Church of Jesus Christ of Latter-day Saints (Strangite), Church of Jesus Christ (Cutlerite), Church of Christ (Temple Lot), The Church of Jesus Christ (Bickerton), and the Fundamentalists.)

Ministers' Salaries

Mormons pride themselves on the fact that all of their people serve without being paid. (This is not true, but it is what they want you to believe.) They call ministers of the gospel "priests of hire" because they receive a salary. They will ask you how your minister is paid. There is a good response to this.

Mormon: How do your ministers get paid? (They want you

to say that your ministers receive a salary so they can say that the ministers are in it for the money.)

Christian: Our ministers are supported like it says in the Bible.

M: How are they supported?

C: I just told you—like it says in the Bible. I thought you had read the Bible! If you would study the Bible you would see exactly what it teaches on this subject. You should read the Bible more carefully. (To see what the New Testament says on this subject, read 1 Corinthians 9:9, 13–14; Galatians 6:6; 1 Timothy 5:18.)

The Priesthood

Mormons believe in two priesthoods: the Aaronic priesthood (concerned with business matters) and the Melchizedek priesthood (responsible for spiritual matters). The Melchizedek priesthood has the most authority. The LDS Church believes that through these priesthoods they get "authority." Mormons will sometimes ask Christians if they have "the priesthood." Don't respond with a detailed theological explanation of how the priesthood was done away with in Christ and how we no longer need any earthly priesthood. Though true, it doesn't help, because it falls on deaf ears.

There is a better answer to give to the LDS missionary—who is just trying to "trap" you. Tell him that Bible-believing Christians believe in two priesthoods: the "Royal" priesthood (1 Peter 2:9) and the "Holy" priesthood (1 Peter 2:5). In most cases, the Mormon you are talking with will not know what to say, so he will move on to another subject.

A Living Prophet

Mormons teach that in the early days the church was ruled by prophets (it was not). They feel that because the man at the head of the LDS organization is called "the prophet," their church is the only true church—since they *alone* have a "living prophet."

(However, most non-Biblically based religious groups have an equivalent of the Mormon prophet! Two examples are: the pope of the Roman Catholic Church and Mr. Moon of the Unification Church.)

When I am asked if my group has a "living prophet," I answer "Yes." They are usually quite surprised because they have been taught that only the LDS Church has a living prophet. They will usually question me about this fact. I say, "Yes indeed, the church I belong to has a living prophet. In fact, He is called 'prophet,' 'priest,' and 'king.'" The Mormons I am talking to may not realize who I am talking about and will continue to question me. I tell them that there is a vast difference between the prophet I am talking about and the one who is the head of the LDS Church. I emphasize the fact that I can go to my prophet at any time of the day or night, and He will listen. In fact, I am invited to come to Him often. This is a privilege that Mormons do not have with their prophet!

I explain to them that *my* prophet—Jesus Christ—is omniscient, omnipotent, and omnipresent, but that their prophet is a mere man who makes many mistakes and has no assurance of where he will go when he dies. I then tell them that my prophet is the Lord Jesus Christ, who knows every detail about His church and His people. Hence He never makes a mistake in the guidance of His church. This will usually end the conversation about prophets.

Faith Without Works Is Dead!

James 2:20 reads: "But wilt thou know, O vain man, that faith without works is dead?" This is a verse that is quoted quite often by Mormons. When they bring up this verse, I startle them by replying: "I agree with this verse 100%. I think faith and works are both very important. I believe and teach that works ought to follow faith. In fact, if you look at this verse you will note that 'faith' comes before 'works.' We need to determine what 'faith' is before we can determine what 'works' are, because works come out of faith. Would you mind showing me from the Bible what this 'faith' is that James is preaching about?" Mormons will declare that they believe that a person needs faith; but in most cases they have no idea what this "faith" is. Their religion is one of "works."

So, I will show them James 2:19, which reads: "Thou believeth that there is one God; thou doest well. The devils also believe, and tremble." I point out to them that this verse says that one of the beliefs which must be included in saving faith is that there is only "one" God. I then ask if the LDS Church believes in only "one" God.

Even though the Mormons believe in many gods, they might answer, "Yes, we believe in one God."

I ask them to explain that statement, as "I have heard that the LDS Church believes in many gods." They will usually admit that they believe in many gods—but will declare that there is only one God with whom they have to do. I say to them: "I understand that Mormons believe that the Father, Jesus Christ, and the Holy Spirit are separate gods." Then I will ask, "If you have to do with only one god, which of these three gods are you talking about?" In the Mormon religion all three play a part, so it will be hard for them to choose only one.

At that point I go back to the original question. I say, "Faith is very important. We have seen that a person must believe that there is only one God. Since Latter-day Saints do not teach this, the Church does not teach a correct, Biblical faith. Until we have agreed about Biblical faith, how can we discuss the subject of works?"

Chapter Nine

Mormon Tactics

THE Mormons use certain tactics to try to catch Christians off guard and make them feel that they (the Mormons) are just another branch of Christianity. Mormons like to present themselves as "Christianity plus." Their goal is to make people think they not only believe like other Christians but have *more* than other Christians. If you are aware of some of these tactics you will be a far more effective witness.

• • •

1. PRAYER. Mormon missionaries will ask if they may pray with you, often at the beginning of your conversation. I know this will happen, so I tell them *I* would like to start off with prayer. (Do not preach in your prayer, but ask the Lord's guidance.) They like to pray also at the end of the session, so close with prayer before they ask. It is best not to let them pray, because they sound very pious when they pray. This tends to deceive people into thinking they are sincere. However, their prayers are memorized and most Mormons will pray the same prayers. Be firm in not letting them pray in your home. *You* do the praying.

Furthermore, they do not pray to the God of the Bible. The god of the Mormons is a god of eternal progression who used to be a sinful man, who has many wives with physical bodies like himself, and who is still continuing to increase in wisdom and knowledge.

. . .

2. TESTIFYING. Mormons are constantly "testifying" about one thing or another. They will testify that almost everything they tell you is true. (In their instruction manual on how to proselytize they are told exactly where to "testify.") You may wonder, as I used to, how anyone can testify to something so strongly without being able to prove what they say. You will find that they have not investigated what they are telling you, it is just part of their memorized speech.

As soon as possible after they "testify" about something, stop them and ask the following question. "I heard you use the word 'testify.' I want to understand exactly what you are saying so that I won't make any mistakes. What do you mean when you use the word 'testify'? Did you use it in the sense that it is something you have studied out very carefully yourself and could prove in a court of law, or are you using it in the sense that you think it is true but can't prove it?"

They will not want to give a clear-cut answer, but keep pressing them until they do. They will have to admit that it is only their opinion or something that was just passed on to them without an iota of personal investigation. By doing this at the beginning you will take a lot of "thunder" out of the rest of their presentation.

. . .

3. "PRAY ABOUT IT." One of the strongest arguments that the Mormons have used to their advantage is to ask you to "pray about it." They are not interested in looking into the truth about Mormonism, examining the many proofs of its errors. One time I was talking to two Mormon missionaries about the first vision that Joseph Smith is said to have had. I mentioned to them that the present story is far different from the original. One of them

said to me, "Prove it, prove it!" I thought he was sincere, so I brought out proof and tried to show him. To my surprise, he would not even look at it. I have had this happen many times since then. Very few will look at the proof, even if it is from an authentic LDS publication.

Because there is such a mountain of evidence that proves Mormonism is false, the LDS hierarchy does not want their people to even consider the facts. The leaders tell the people that all they have to do is pray about their history or teachings to know if it is true or not. They don't need to investigate. The implication is that they will *always* get a good feeling about the things they pray about. This is supposed to make it "the truth." They will tell you very plainly, "I don't care what the facts are. As long as I have a 'good feeling' about it, that is enough for me." The idea that one should ignore all the facts for an indescribable feeling that is supposed to come through prayer is hard to comprehend. However, the Mormons have heard this line for so long that they have fallen for it.

It doesn't matter what you are talking about, the Mormons will always begin to press you to "pray about it" and especially about *The Book of Mormon*. If you ignore them or go to another subject they will imply that you are afraid to pray about it. They continually keep coming back to this one subject. They will quote two verses found in *The Book of Mormon* in Moroni 10:3–4 (page 529), which reads:

> Behold, I would exhort you that when ye shall read these things, if it be wisdom in God that ye should read them, that ye would remember how merciful the Lord hath been unto the children of men, from the creation of Adam even down unto the time that ye shall receive these things, and ponder it in your hearts. And when ye shall receive these things, I would exhort you that ye would ask God, the Eternal Father, in the name of Christ, if these things are not true; and if ye shall ask with a sincere heart, with

real intent, having faith in Christ, he will manifest the truth of it unto you, by the power of the Holy Ghost.

The intent of this passage is that if you are "sincere" you will always get a good feeling (even though they can never give you any idea of what this feeling is to be like). The implication is that if you do not get "a feeling" then you are not "sincere." They will often challenge you to pray about *The Book of Mormon*, and the next time they come will ask you about it. Even if a person does pray about it, if he doesn't get some kind of feeling the Mormons will say, "I am greatly disappointed in you. I thought that you were really 'sincere.' But why don't you pray about it again and see if you do not get the 'feeling'?" The average person does not want to be thought of as being insincere, so the next time he will at least say that he got some kind of a feeling. This is the first big step—and a dangerous one—toward accepting the story of Joseph Smith as God's Prophet. This tactic has probably gotten more people into Mormonism than any other.

It is very important that you gain the victory at this point because it will take most of the thunder out of the rest of the elders' presentation. There are several ways that you can show them how foolish it is to "just pray about *The Book of Mormon*" and supposedly get a "good feeling," which in reality is to prove that all of Mormonism is true. Here are five different approaches that I have used to get them to question this principle of "just pray about it." You might need only one or you might need to use all of them before your sessions with the elders are completed.

(1) "Which version of *The Book of Mormon* should I pray about? Should I pray about the 1830 original *Book of Mormon*, about one of the several revised versions made down through the years, or about the present edition of *The Book of Mormon*? After all, there are at least 3,913 changes that have been made in *The*

Book of Mormon." (Usually the Mormons you are talking with will reply that these changes are only in punctuation and spelling.) These revisions are *not* just in punctuation and spelling, for many of the changes alter and subvert the whole meaning.

However, if what the Mormons have said about the "bringing forth" of *The Book of Mormon* is true, there should have been no need for *any* changes. There are a number of accounts concerning this in official Mormon writings, and I will quote from two of them.

The first is from a published speech by David Whitmer, who was one of the three witnesses to *The Book of Mormon.*

> I will now give you a description of the manner in which the *Book of Mormon* was translated. Joseph Smith would put the seer stone into a hat, and put his face in the hat, drawing it closely around his face to exclude the light; and in the darkness the spiritual light would shine. A piece of something resembling parchment would appear, and on that appeared the writing. One character at a time would appear, and under it was the interpretation in English. (*An Address To All Believers in Christ*, by David Whitmer, p. 12.)

This second quote is probably the best and the most detailed. It is recorded in the journal of Oliver B. Huntington. He is referring to a talk given by Joseph F. Smith, who became the sixth president of the Mormon church, saying that the Lord gave Joseph Smith the exact English wording and spelling that he should use in *The Book of Mormon.*

> Saturday Feb. 25, 1881, I went to Provo to a quarterly Stake Conference. Heard Joseph F. Smith describe the manner of translating the *Book of Mormon* by Joseph Smith the Prophet and Seer, which was as follows as near as I can recollect the substance of his description. JOSEPH DID NOT RENDER THE WRITING ON THE GOLD PLATES INTO THE ENGLISH LANGUAGE

IN HIS OWN STYLE OR LANGUAGE as many people believe, BUT EVERY WORD AND EVERY LETTER was given to him by the gift and power of God. So it is the work of God and not of Joseph Smith, and it was done in this way. . . . .THE LORD CAUSED EACH WORD SPELLED AS IT IS IN THE BOOK TO APPEAR ON THE STONES IN SHORT SENTENCES OR WORDS, and when Joseph had uttered the sentence or word before him and the scribe had written it properly, that sentence would disappear and another appear. AND IF THERE WAS A WORD WRONGLY WRITTEN OR EVEN A LETTER IN-CORRECT the writing of the stones would remain there. Then Joseph would require the scribe to spell the reading of the last spoken word and thus find the mistake, and when corrected the sentence would disappear as usual. [Emphases added.] (Journal of Oliver B. Huntington, p. 168 of typed copy at Utah State Historical Society.)

However, in recent years a few thinking Mormons have realized that such statements would make God responsible for the mistakes in grammar and spelling. Thus Mormons have tried to get around this by saying that the printer made some changes. The only problem is, the publisher wanted to correct some of the spelling and grammar but those working with Joseph Smith on the publishing of *The Book of Mormon* would not let him do so.

Of course, the Mormons have tried to play down the changes that have been made in *The Book of Mormon*, but some of them are very important. In fact, one of the changes is probably concerning the greatest fact in the whole world.

The original *Book of Mormon* taught that there was a Trinity (a truth they completely deny today) made up of only one God. In the original *Book of Mormon*, in Mormon 7:7b (page 531) it says,

> "...to sing ceaseless praise unto the choirs above, unto the Father, and unto the Son, and unto the Holy Ghost, which *is* one God, in a state of happiness which hath no end."

In the present edition of *The Book of Mormon*, on page 471, this verse has been changed to read,

"...which *are* one God."

This change gives them three distinct and separate gods (which in reality is in contradiction to the rest of *The Book of Mormon*) but helps the verse to conform to the LDS belief that there are many gods. (I know that "which are one God" is not proper English, but this is the way it is now written.)

Four important changes in *The Book of Mormon* are concerning the Godhead. These changes were apparently made to support the doctrine of a plurality of Gods. The first is in 1 Nephi 13:40; page 32 in the 1830 original edition reads as follows:

". . . These last records . . . shall make known to all kindreds, tongues, and people, that the Lamb of God is the Eternal Father and the Savior. . . ."

In the present edition, on page 25, it reads:

". . . These last records . . . shall make known to all kindreds, tongues, and people, that the Lamb of God is THE SON OF the Eternal Father, and the Savior. . . ."

The second alteration is found in 1 Nephi 11:18, on page 25 of the original 1830 edition.

". . . Behold, the virgin which thou seest, is the Mother of GOD, after the manner of the flesh."

In the modern edition, on page 18, it reads:

". . . Behold, the virgin whom thou seest is the mother of THE SON OF GOD, after the manner of the flesh."

The third revision is in 1 Nephi 11:21, on page 25 in the original, which reads:

> "And the angel said unto me, behold the Lamb of God, yea, even THE ETERNAL FATHER!"

In the 1964 edition, on page 19, it reads:

> "And the angel said unto me: Behold the Lamb of God, yea, even THE SON OF the Eternal Father!"

The fourth statement is found in 1 Nephi 11:32, on page 26 of the 1830 original edition.

> ". . . the Everlasting God, was judged of the world; and I saw and bear record."

In the present edition, on page 19, it has been changed to:

> ". . . the SON OF THE everlasting God was judged of the world; and I saw and bear record."

One of the most amazing changes in *The Book of Mormon*, however, is the one found in Alma 29:4. Some very important words have been left out. This verse in the 1830 original edition, on page 303, reads:

> ". . . yea, I know that he allotteth unto men, YEA DECREETH UNTO THEM DECREES WHICH ARE UNALTERABLE, according to their wills: . . ."

But in the present edition, on page 267, the eight highlighted words have been left out. We find out that what was supposed to be "decrees which are unalterable" have been "altered."

"...yea, I know that he allotteth unto men according to their wills,..."

When Mormons tell you that there have been only unimportant, minor changes in *The Book of Mormon*—in punctuation, spelling and grammar only—they do not know what they are talking about.*

So you should say to your visitor: "In determining the accuracy of any old writings, it is generally taken that the one which is closest to the original is the most accurate; hence, if a person is to pray about *The Book of Mormon* then it clearly ought to be about the original one. In your case [addressed to the Mormon you are talking to], did you specifically pray about the original *Book of Mormon*?" (He probably never even prayed at all about *The Book of Mormon* let alone making a distinction between the original and the present edition.) The elders will try to assure you that it really doesn't make any difference, but you should insist that it *does* make a lot of difference. Ask them if they would be willing to get a copy of the original *Book of Mormon* and go through and check out the 3,913 changes to see if there have not been some very *important* changes made between the original and the present edition.

They will probably tell you again that it really is not important and that they are too busy on their mission and don't have time to check it out. Point out the fact to them that they have to be specific as to which *Book of Mormon* they want you to believe in because if the present edition is correct, then the original, which was supposedly directly translated by God from the gold plates, is incorrect; and if the original one is correct, then some man has

---

* I have personally discovered that when *The Book of Mormon* was translated into Japanese, even further liberties were taken with the text—in an effort, seemingly, to make parts of it conform more to LDS doctrine. The same could be true of other foreign translations, though I can't say so with certainty.

changed the book—because there are so many contradictions and changes between the two.

(2) "What if I prayed and got a 'bad' feeling? Would that mean that *The Book of Mormon* is not a book from God and that you are mistaken?" They will probably insist that this could never happen. But you can say to them, "If I am sincere, you say that I will always get a 'good feeling.' How can you determine that beforehand? Are you claiming to be certified prognosticators? How can you predict before a person prays what the outcome will be? Obviously, it doesn't do a person any good to pray! If I go by what you say, there can be no reason for my praying at all! You can't give me any idea of the kind of feeling I am supposed to get, and now you tell me that I am sure to get it—so I can't see that this is any kind of test at all. It seems like you are telling me that only Mormons are 'sincere' and everyone else in the world is *insincere*. How can you make such a bigoted and boastful statement!"

(3) "Why just pray about *The Book of Mormon*? Since I ought to be 'sincere' and not have a closed mind, then why should not you and I pray about all the various religious books in the world— like the *Quran* of the Muslims, the *Divine Principles* of the Unification Church, and the multiplied books of the Watchtower Society of the Jehovah Witnesses? Or let's pray about the Bible alone, which born-again Christians truly believe." (I am in no way saying that the other religions might be right and that you can determine this by prayer, but am attempting to show the Mormons just how foolish their hypothesis is and trying to get them to do some serious thinking.) They will probably insist that it is not necessary to pray about the other books since they are sure they are wrong. However, you can invert their argument and suggest that they are afraid to check out other religions and books. This shows they are not really "sincere" and have very closed minds.

(4) "What if I really wanted to be 'sincere' and obey the clear commands of the Bible in Deuteronomy 13:14a and, as a result, I begin to 'inquire, and make search, and ask diligently' about *The Book of Mormon*—and thereby discover that there are some serious problems in it? Should I still press ahead and pray about the book, in spite of all the flaws my investigation has revealed; or should I continue to be *genuinely* sincere and seek some kind of logical answers rather than pray about it?" If they insist that you just go ahead and "pray about it," then you can point out that their religion is wholly based on some kind of an "indescribable feeling" and not on proven facts. It is dangerous to believe the word of two complete strangers (which the Mormon missionaries are), who are usually just 19 or 20 years of age, without checking out what they have to say. After all, the Bible does warn that there will be many false teachers of religion in the world.

(5) I will ask the Mormons I am speaking with if this "pray about it" test applies *just* to *The Book of Mormon* or if it applies to other matters as well. They will probably say that you can pray about other matters also.

When I get this kind of response, before the Mormons come the next time I will take a book, preferably the King James Bible (which is the one they use) and put it in a paper bag or some other wrapping that can't been seen through. (I happen to have the *Inspired Version* of the Bible which Joseph Smith allegedly purified from the many mistakes which he claimed the Bible contains, so I have even put *it* inside.) When the elders arrive, I set the parcel before them, but will not let them look inside. Then I say, "You told me that you could determine the truthfulness of certain matters by 'praying about it.' Will you pray over the book that is in this bag and tell me if it is a book of truth or of error?" They will usually stammer a little and then say, "We can't pray about it until we first know what is inside. We will have to scan the contents of the book first, and then read it carefully to see if it is worth praying about." I will then reply, "Thank you very much. I will take your advice and study *The Book of Mormon* and thereby determine if it is worth praying about or not, so please don't ask me anymore to pray about *The Book of Mormon* or any other matter until I have thoroughly investigated it." This is usually the end of the "pray about it" test.

• • •

4. THEIR CLAIM TO BE THE ONLY CHURCH THAT HAS A LIVING PROPHET AS THEIR LEADER. Mormons testify that Joseph Smith was a true prophet, and that the current president of the LDS Church is also a prophet of God. At this point I ask them, "Did I understand what you said? Did you say that you *know* that the current president of the Mormon Church is a true prophet of God?" They will state that they do.

I continue by saying, "Let me test what you said. The test of a true prophet is found in Deuteronomy 18:20–22. When a true prophet prophesies something, it will be fulfilled exactly as prophesied. The test is simple but very important." Then I say to them, "Would you kindly relate three specific prophecies of major importance that the current president of the church has given and tell me how and when they were fulfilled. Three isn't very many, so it should be easy for you to give me examples!"

They will not be able to give you any valid prophecies. I respond by saying, "I am really disappointed! You assured me that the current president of the church was a true prophet, even though you have no basis upon which to make such a statement. How can I believe that claim?"

Chapter Ten

Ways Mormons Attack the Christian Faith

MORMONS would like to make people think they are "Christianity plus." However, they attack the traditional Christian faith and try to leave the impression that some important teachings have been taken away, changed, or corrupted, and they have restored and corrected these elements. If you are aware of some of their tactics and false claims and have a ready answer, you will be a much more effective witness.

• • •

1. AUTHORITY. For many years the Mormons have been asking non-Mormons, "Where do you get your authority?" The Mormons are taught that the LDS Church of Salt Lake City, Utah, is the only church that has the authority to "act for God." They claim that the authority of their priesthood was given to Joseph Smith and that this authority was necessary to organize and carry on the church. They believe that this authority has been passed from Joseph Smith to the continuing leaders of the church. They maintain that all who hold either the Aaronic or Melchizedek priesthood, or both, have certain powers that were delegated to them. Mormons are not aware of the Biblical teach-

ing that ministers of the gospel have been called directly by Jesus Christ and have been ordained by Him. Thus, when they ask you where your group gets its authority, you should point them to Matthew 28:18–20 and tell them that it comes from Jesus Christ.

•   •   •

2. BIBLICAL "MISTAKES." It is quite common for Mormon missionaries to carry a King James Bible with them. This does not mean that they believe what is written in it. They will quote verses from it to try to prove some of their teachings.

One of the 13 articles of faith of the LDS Church is "We believe the Bible to be the Word of God as far as it is translated correctly; we also believe *The Book of Mormon* to be the Word of God." This sounds good on the surface, but in reality they believe that only a small part of the Bible is translated correctly. They claim that many precious truths have been taken away from the Bible through many translations into different languages so that it can no longer be relied upon.

(1) You can point out that this is a strange statement because so many verses and chapters in *The Book of Mormon* are *exactly* like those in the King James Bible, which is the one they use. If all the verses copied from the Bible were taken out of *The Book of Mormon,* a large portion of it would be gone. If there are really so many mistakes in the Bible, then there are also many mistakes in *The Book of Mormon*!

(2) Ask the Mormons you are dealing with, "If there are so many mistakes in the Bible, why don't you use the *Inspired Version*?" (From June 1830 to July 2, 1833, Joseph Smith went through the King James Bible and changed it to suit himself. However, 90% of this "revision" is exactly the same as the King James Version. This altered edition of the Bible is known as the *Inspired Version*.) The Mormons will probably not know what you are talking about. If you explain that the *Inspired Version* and

the *Joseph Smith Translation* are the same, they will probably understand, but will reply by saying that it was never completed, so that is why they don't use it. But it *was* completed, as shown from the following quotes.

In the July 1833 issue of the *Evening and Morning Star*, the official Mormon newspaper at that time, Joseph Smith wrote:

> As to the errors in the bible, any man possessed with common understanding knows that both the old and new testaments are filled with errors, obscurities, italics and contradictions, which must be the work of men. As the church of Christ will soon have the scriptures in their original purity, it may not be amiss for us to show a few of the gross errors, or, as they might be termed, contradictions.

In another Mormon-published newspaper, *Times and Seasons*, Vol. 6, page 802 (as bound), Joseph Smith quoted an article that he wrote on July 2, 1833: "We are exceedingly fatigued owing to a great press of business. We this day finished the translation of the scriptures, for which we return gratitude to our Heavenly Father." You will note that this agrees with the time he promised he would complete it in the previous quote. Joseph Smith claimed God commanded him to translate it and *publish* it. (See *Doctrine and Covenants* 35:20; 42:56–57; and 45:57–62. The Mormons you are conversing with will have a copy of the *Doctrine and Covenants* and could easily look up these passages.) If the translation was *not* finished (the evidence shows otherwise) and *not* printed, then Joseph Smith was disobedient to the command of God! I don't know what other conclusion one can reach.

After Joseph Smith died and Brigham Young took control of the movement there was a squabble over leadership, leading to a split, and the Smith faction started the Reorganized Church of Jesus Christ of Latter-day Saints. Joseph's wife, Emma, was a member of this group, and she had possession of the manuscript to this translation of the Bible. The Reorganized Church had it printed in December 1867 and it is still available.

The Mormons have a book containing the four standard works of the Mormons, including the King James Version of the Bible. In this Bible they have added "explanatory notes." These annotations make many references to Joseph Smith's Translation, abbreviated as JST. The Bible they are carrying has notes about this translation as far along as Revelation 20:6. In order to prove to the elders that Joseph Smith really did finish this translation, ask them to turn in the Bible they have to Revelation 20:6 and look at the note where it mentions the JST version. (If you forget the exact verse, ask them to look at the latter part of the Book of Revelation and see if they can't find a reference to the JST rendering, of which there are many.) As we all know, Revelation is the last book of the Bible. If Joseph Smith did not finish his translation, how can they print footnotes from an uncompleted Bible? The Mormons can't use Smith's full translation today because many of the current teachings of the Mormon church directly contradict it. Furthermore, they can deceive more people by using the King James Version than they can by using Joseph Smith's Translation.

Remind your visitors of Joseph Smith's promise to "purify" the Bible. Point out that it is foolish for them to read the "corrupted" (according to Joseph Smith) King James Version, even one with footnotes in it, when they have a purified Bible! (Presenting these facts should show them that LDS leaders are not telling them the truth.)

*   *   *

3. THE BIBLE AND "MISSING" SCRIPTURES. Mormons claim to believe certain verses even while doing all they can to destroy a person's confidence in the Bible. One of the ways that they do this is to claim that there are at least 15 books missing from the Bible. They point to the following books mentioned in

the Bible: the Book of the Covenant (Exodus 24:7), the Book of the Wars of the Lord (Numbers 21:14), the Book of Jasher (Joshua 10:13), the Book of the Acts of Solomon (1 Kings 11:41), and others. They imply that these books used to be part of the Bible. They use this to try to prove that much of the Bible is missing. They also cite John 21:25, which says, "And there are also many other things which Jesus did, the which if they should be written every one, I suppose that even the world itself could not contain the books that should be written. Amen." They imply from this that there were a number of New Testament books that no longer exist. This is not what that verse says. It only states that the world would not be able to contain all the books *if* the many things that Jesus did were written down.

The Bible-believing Christian knows that God has preserved His Word in its entirety. You can explain that Jesus set His approval upon all of the Old Testament, that the Old Testament is quoted many hundreds of times in the New Testament, *and* that all of the references are found in our Old Testament. Also, we have many quotes from the Bible in the writings of the early Church Fathers and all of these quoted passages exist in our Bible today. However, this kind of an argument likely won't impress the Mormons, so I suggest you say to them: "You feel that you cannot rely on the Bible because a number of books supposedly are missing." They will usually agree. Then say: "Let's look at *The Book of Mormon* for a few minutes. What happened to the first 116 pages of *The Book of Mormon* known as the "Book of Lehi"?

The "Book of Lehi" is the original opening section of *The Book of Mormon* written by Joseph Smith. A rich farmer in the area where Joseph Smith lived had promised to finance the publication of this "Golden Book." The farmer's wife was not happy about this and wanted to read part of the book before she would give her approval. Smith was reluctant at first, but finally he let Martin Harris have the 116 pages that he had written. Harris's wife either hid the manuscript or destroyed it. Since Smith had produced only that one copy, he could not rewrite it exactly like the first. If Joseph had rewritten the manuscript, someone might have produced the original copy and people would have seen the difference. (Remember, Joseph Smith was supposed to be translating this material infallibly from gold plates.) Therefore Joseph Smith said, very conveniently, that he had received a revelation from God not to translate the 116 pages again. (See *Doctrine and Covenants*, Section 10, verse 30.) So these 116 pages, one-fifth of *The Book of Mormon,* are missing.

The Mormon elders will probably tell you that Joseph Smith received a revelation not to rewrite the missing pages.

Reply: "This seems rather strange. You were just telling me that because there are a number of books that are supposedly missing from the Bible you do not have confidence in it. There is no evidence that these books you mention were ever among the canonical books of the Bible. But from officially recognized LDS writings there is proof that the 116 pages of the "Book of Lehi" were intended to be part of *The Book of Mormon.* These 116 pages actually existed. Yet the fact that one-fifth of *The Book of Mormon* is missing doesn't seem to shake your confidence in *The Book of Mormon*! This does not add up to me!"

· · ·

4. CHRIST DIED ONLY FOR REPENTED SINS. The Mormons laugh at the idea that Christ died for *all* our sins, past, present, and future. They claim that Christ died only for the sins of which we repent.

Here are some questions you can ask concerning this Mormon belief.

(1) "I don't understand what you are saying. According to the Bible, sin can be in word, thought, or deed. It is a sin to know that you ought to do good but don't do it (James 4:17). There are many good things that we should do and yet don't. How are

we going to repent of sins of which we are not aware?"

(2) "There are over 1,100 commandments in the Bible. It is impossible to know all of these commandments, let alone obey them."

(3) "I have heard that Mormons teach that it takes a long time to repent. Mormons must be spending all their time in repenting!"

(4) "If a person really repents, he will not go out and commit the same sin over again. This means that you can repent of a sin only once. [I am speaking from the Mormon point of view here.] Do you mean to tell me that you have never committed the same sin twice? It would be impossible for us to repent of our sins one by one."

(5) "What would happen if you committed a sin like adultery but died before you could repent of that sin? You would not have obtained God's forgiveness for this sin, so wouldn't you have to suffer for it through all eternity?"

(6) "To me, this idea of having to repent of every individual sin before it is forgiven has a lot of problems. [Give them an opportunity to respond.] I think the solution found in the Bible is much better. 1 John 1:7 reads: 'The blood of Jesus Christ, his Son, cleanseth us from all sin.' I know that all of my sins have been forgiven because of the death of Christ on the cross for me."

• • •

5. A CONTENTIOUS SPIRIT. As long as you sit quietly, listen, and agree with what the Mormons say, there is no problem. They will stay as long as they possibly can. However, if you begin to ask well-thought-out questions or point out contradictions in what they have said, they will accuse you of having "a contentious spirit."

My reply is: "If I am contentious it is because the Bible commands me to be so. The Bible clearly tells me that I am not to believe every religious group that comes my way. I am told to 'test' (1 John 4:1–3) all religions according to the Bible. Deuteronomy 13 is a chapter which talks about testing any group which claims that they have a prophet. In verse 14 it says: 'Then shalt thou inquire, and make search, and ask diligently. . . .' [This is a good verse to know.] This is the extent to which I am to test a religion. You mean to tell me that because I am obeying the clear command of the Bible to 'inquire, and make search, and ask diligently' I am being contentious?" (In most cases they won't have a reply.)

• • •

6. EXALTATION. Mormons talk about "exaltation," by which they mean *becoming a god.* They teach that "godhood" can be achieved by good works and effort as prescribed by the Mormon church.

The best answer to this claim is to ask them to name *all* the requirements for becoming a god. Through my research I have come up with at least fifteen requirements that must be met to become a Mormon god, which are:

(1) Faith.

(2) Repentance.

(3) Baptism by someone with the proper LDS authority.

(4) Laying on of hands for the gift of the Holy Spirit.

(5) Obeying the law of chastity.

(6) Obeying the law of tithing.

(7) Obeying the "Word of Wisdom," which means no coffee, tea, tobacco, or alcohol.

(8) A person must obey all the commandments of their scriptures.

(9) Must be married in the temple for time and eternity. Also must have children sealed to them for eternity.

(10) Must actively perform baptisms for the dead.

(11) Must practice polygamy. (Mormons believe this will be

reinstated during the Millennium.)

(12) Must be in complete subjection to everything the church authorities say.

(13) Must believe that Joseph Smith was a true prophet of God and that the present-day president of the church is also a true prophet of God.

(14) Must spend two years as a missionary for the church.

(15) Must not practice any kind of birth control.

I have never met a Mormon who knew even one half of these requirements. (I once was in a long correspondence with one of the 21 assistants to the apostles of the LDS Church but he could not name the requirements for me.) Since they don't know the qualifications for godhood, it would be impossible for them to *promise* anyone they could become a god. The Mormons might reply that these will be revealed to you as you progress. But you can point out to them the danger of starting and then finding out that you cannot meet the requirements: all your efforts will have been in vain. (We know that it is impossible for any sinful human being to work his way to being a god, but even among the Mormons who teach such a thing, less than 5% of their membership have made any effort to try and fulfill the stipulations, and most don't know all that is required.)

• • •

7. LATTER-DAY FALLING AWAY. The Mormons talk about a "falling away." They teach that around 400 A.D. the church completely fell away from New Testament principles and practices. They claim this made necessary the restoration of the gospel, and this was done through Joseph Smith. They point to verses in the Bible which speak about an anticipated falling away.

As long as we have the Bible and submit to its authority, there cannot be a "complete" falling away of the true church. Jesus Christ began the church and He is going to keep it to the very end.

However, it can be proven by Mormon teachings that there was *not* a "complete" falling away. The Mormon church teaches that as long as there is one "apostle" living there will not be a falling away. They also say that the Apostle John never died and is living somewhere today (See *Doctrine and Covenants,* section 7, especially the explanation at the beginning of the section). Thus there could not have been a complete falling away as the LDS Church claims, and hence there is no need for a restoration.

· · ·

8. LYING. The Mormons will not always tell you the truth, nor will they tell you what they actually believe. They only tell you what they want you to hear and when they want you to hear it. Sometimes they lie out of ignorance—or it might be Mormon "double talk." However, I have had them deliberately lie to me. I have asked elders about a doctrine that they believe and have had them deny that they believed or taught such a thing, almost with an oath. When I reacted by showing them from their own writings that Mormons truly *do* believe what I stated, they then admitted that this indeed is what they believe—without any embarrassment or apology.

· · ·

9. PERFECTION. It may seem strange, but Mormons will often quote Matthew 5:48: "Be ye therefore perfect, even as your Father which is in heaven is perfect." Why? Because they believe that they can become perfect by their own good works. If you tell them this is impossible, they will reply, "Why would God command something that is impossible?" Born-again believers, of course, know that no one can attain perfection by *his own* good works, but Mormons do not understand this point.

When they use this verse, I suggest that you ask them if Matthew 5:48 is a *present* or *future* command. If they say it is a *present* command, ask if they are perfect before God at this very moment. They will answer, "Of course not, but I'm striving to be."

Point out to them that they are not obeying the commandments of the Bible if they are not *currently* perfect. Merely "striving" is not adequate, and the imperfect person cannot enter the kingdom of God.

If they state that it is a *future* command, point out the verses that speak of some people being "perfect" in this life. Genesis 6:9 declares: "These are the generations of Noah: Noah was a just man and perfect in his generations, and Noah walked with God." Noah was in some sense "perfect," so it is possible to be perfect before God right *now*. (See 1 Kings 8:61; 15:14; Job 1:1; Psalm 37:37.)

Press on and stress the fact that the Bible requires *all* men to be perfect, either by a flawless record of good works or in the same sense that Noah was perfect. Ask the Mormons why *they* are not obeying this commandment. They will undoubtedly ask you if *you* are perfect! Take this opportunity to present the gospel to them: Explain that all men are sinners; even our best works are imperfect before God. Jesus is the *only* one who lived a perfect life on earth. We can be made perfect only through the blood of Christ which He shed on the cross. If we put our faith in Him as our Lord and Savior, we are instantly declared righteous—blameless in Him. Our lives will then progress and mature towards actual perfection in Him, which will ultimately be realized fully when we are with Him in heaven.

• • •

10. INTIMIDATION. Mormons may be sweet and kind when you first meet them, and will continue so if you listen meekly and agree with everything they say. However, if you ask them thought-provoking questions they become frustrated and resort to special tactics to get you off course. It is good to know what these tactics are.

(1) They will tell you to hold out your hand, to see if you are trembling. Even if your hand is as steady as possible, they will

still accuse you of being nervous. They say that this is caused by the devil that is in you.

(2) Frequently they will say, "I command you. . . ."

(3) They may call down the curse of God upon you. They are apt to be very dramatic! It is only a trick.

(4) If you don't believe what they say, they may accuse you of being insincere, contentious, etc.

Chapter Eleven

Facts About
The Book of Mormon

The Book of Mormon Contains the Fullness of the Gospel

When Mormon missionaries first approach you, they emphasize and praise *The Book of Mormon*. They state that it contains the fullness of the gospel and is the keystone of their religion. Joseph Smith made the following remark: "I told the brethren that *The Book of Mormon* was the most correct of any book on earth and the keystone of our religion, and a man would get nearer to God by abiding by its precepts than by any other book" (*Teachings of the Prophet Joseph Smith*, p. 194).

The *Doctrine and Covenants* 42:12 also says, "And again, the elders, priests, and teachers of this church shall teach the principles of my gospel, which are in the Bible and *The Book of Mormon*, in the which is the fullness of the gospel."

Actually, *The Book of Mormon* is one of the most anti-Mormon books that I know. None of the basic doctrines taught by the LDS Church can be found in it. In fact, most of what is found in the book is just the opposite of what Mormon's think it teaches. The Mormons use *The Book of Mormon* as a bridge to get people from the Bible to real Mormon teachings, which are found only in their other books. If a person read *The Book of Mormon* and accepted its spiritual teachings (it contains stories of many wars and lots of other material that is completely irrelevant to one's spiritual needs), taking them at face value, he would turn out to be a Campbellite, or one who believes in "the baptism of regeneration."

However, you can make use of their laudatory statements concerning *The Book of Mormon* and put them to your advantage in witnessing. You should say something like: "Since you feel that *The Book of Mormon* is such a wonderful book and is the 'keystone of your religion,' as Joseph Smith stated, I would like you to go through *The Book of Mormon* and show me *all* of your major doctrines and ordinances from it. For example: . . ."

Here is a list of 38 of their major doctrines, but not *one* of them is derived from or can be proved by *The Book of Mormon*.

1. Matter is eternal.
2. God has a body of flesh and bone.
3. God is an exalted man.
4. God is a product of eternal progression.
5. God and his wives gave birth, through physical relations, to spiritual children.
6. God organized the world rather than created it.
7. There are many gods.
8. Man is made in the physical likeness of God.
9. Christ was only the first begotten. He is not God.
10. Jesus was conceived by physical intercourse involving God and Mary.
11. Christ was married and had at least three wives.
12. Christ had children through his marriage.
13. There is no literal eternal hellfire or punishment.
14. Men can become gods. (Women cannot become gods but only the wives of gods.)
15. Intelligence is eternal.

16. Man has a preexisting spirit.
17. Baptism may be performed for the dead.
18. Salvation may be obtained by proxy.
19. Marriage is for time and eternity.
20. Polygamy is not an abomination in the sight of God.
21. Sealing ordinances ensure the celestial continuation of families.
22. There are three degrees of eternal glory.
23. Mankind has a "mother" in heaven.
24. Man will have a second chance after death.
25. There continues to be an Aaronic priesthood consisting of the offices of deacon, teacher, and priest.
26. There continues to be a Melchizedek priesthood consisting of the offices of elder, seventy, and high priest.
27. The authority to baptize came from John the Baptist.
28. The authority to ordain rested only in Peter, James, and John, and was given to men.
29. The church performs temple services, marriage, baptism, etc.
30. The third heaven is divided into three parts and is only for Mormons.
31. People will live as families in heaven.
32. Some preexistent spirits were bad and so were born on earth with darker skin or with black skin.
33. Until June 1978, blacks were to be denied the priesthood.
34. The church's valid and authorized offices are evangelist, bishop, stake president, assistant to the Twelve, First President, and President.
35. All men are resurrected because of the death of Christ but exaltation (becoming a god) is a matter of one's own works.
36. *The Book of Mormon* is the "Stick of Joseph."
37. The law of tithing, chastity, the Word of Wisdom, and the keeping of the teachings and doctrines of the LDS are essential to salvation.
38. Jesus Christ is the Jehovah of the Old Testament.

They will tell you that they can't do this from *The Book of Mormon* and must use all four of their standard works, namely: (1) The Bible (Actually they believe and teach that the Bible is full of mistakes; they state that they "believe the Bible as far as it is translated correctly," but they do not believe very much of it *is* translated correctly! However, they do use many verses they think prove their doctrines, while completely ignoring the rest of its teachings), (2) *The Book of Mormon*, (3) *Doctrine and Covenants*, and (4) *The Pearl of Great Price*. (In reality, not all of their doctrines, ordinances, and practices are taken from these four works. You must also consult the recorded discourses and writings of Joseph Smith and Brigham Young.)

You can point out to them that if LDS doctrines and practices are not found in *The Book of Mormon* then the generations of people who make up the 1000 years of history contained in *The Book of Mormon* could not really have been Mormons! According to Mormon teaching, these people did not have any of the other three works and would only have known the contents of *The Book of Mormon*. Since LDS doctrine is not to be found in *The Book of Mormon*, it is only logical that the Nephites and Lamanites could not be Mormons. It is very strange that the very people who (supposedly) wrote the gold plates from which *The Book of Mormon* is purportedly taken did not have knowledge of and believe Mormon doctrine!

The Source of *The Book of Mormon*

Mormons like to present Joseph Smith as an ignorant farm boy who had little formal education. If you question the source of *The Book of Mormon*, they will say, "How could a person with only a third-grade education write such a marvelous book? The only answer is that it came from God." There are, however, other good answers to this question.

Ask them how much formal education Thomas Edison, Benjamin Franklin, or another well-known person had—one whom you know was only moderately educated.

There are other questions that can be raised about Joseph Smith. If he was such an ignorant farm boy with little education, why was he licensed to start a bank in Kirtland, Ohio, in 1837 and allowed to become the treasurer of that bank? If he was so ignorant when *The Book of Mormon* came forth, why was it that in less than ten years he was elected mayor of Nauvoo? Why did he appoint himself to the Board of Regents for the University of Nauvoo in 1842? How could he produce *The Book of Abraham,* which was incorporated into *The Pearl of Great Price? The Book of Abraham*, was published a few years after *The Book of Mormon* and is written in the same style. It has been proved that the source material—an Egyptian papyrus—that Joseph Smith claims to have translated *The Book of Abraham* from has nothing in common with the book. This clearly makes Joseph Smith the *author* of *The Book of Abraham*. Obviously, Joseph Smith was self-educated. He was an avid reader who retained and built upon what he read.

The Book of Mormon can be traced to two main sources, both of which were available in Smith's day. They are:

1. *The King James Version of the Bible.* In *The Book of Mormon* there are whole chapters copied almost verbatim from the KJV. Chapters 2–14 of Isaiah are largely identical in the KJV to 2 Nephi, chapters 12–24, pages 81–96 in *The Book of Mormon*. Thousands of quotations from the KJV are used. Many of *The Book of Mormon*'s main characters were extracted from the Bible. However, names and circumstances have been changed to cover up this fact. Major portions of *The Book of Mormon* would be missing if all the direct quotes, indirect quotes, and references to incidents in the Bible were deleted from it.

2. *View of the Hebrews* by Ethan Smith (no relation to Joseph Smith). This book was published seven years before *The Book of Mormon* and was printed only 15 miles from where Joseph

Smith lived. It is known that Joseph Smith had a copy of the 1825 reprint of this book because he refers to it by name in his church periodical *Times and Seasons*, Vol. 3, June 1, 1842, page 814. This book teaches that the ten lost tribes of Israel became the American Indians. This was a common belief in the 1800's. Ideas and expressions taken from it are embedded in *The Book of Mormon*. Some honest Mormon writers have acknowledged these similarities and have come to the conclusion that Joseph Smith copied from *View of the Hebrews*. (It is a good idea to have this book on hand when dealing with Mormons. Go through the book and underline the passages that are similar to *The Book of Mormon*. I have shown this book to a number of Mormons and have found that it is very effective. Information on obtaining this book can be found in the Appendix under the heading "Source Material on Mormonism.")

Here is a list of similar things, along with the page numbers, that are found in both *View of the Hebrews*, 1825 2nd Edition (listed first), and *The Book of Mormon* (B.M.).

1. P. 2. Chapter 1. Destruction of Jerusalem. Time 600 B.C. (B.M. P. 1, 1:4.)
2. P. 47. Certain restoration.
3. P. 53. Stick of Judah and Ephraim.
4. Pages 76, 78, 140, & 210. The Great Spirit. (B.M. P. 242. Alma 18:24–28; P. 246. Alma 19:25–27; P. 252. Alma 22:9–11.)
5. P. 79. Jews were the aborigines of the American continent.
6. P. 81. Gives the date of the Exile—the time the Jews were carried away into Babylon. (B.M. P. 1. Date 600 B.C.)
7. P. 83. Lost revelation.
8. P. 114. 2,500 years ago the Hebrews came to America.
9. P. 115. Had a "book."
10. P. 130. Had a "book." Was lost. Will have it again.

11. P. 150. "Urim" and "Thummim." A breastplate. (B.M. Introduction. P. 3.)
12. P. 151. High priest.
13. P. 152. The people in America came from a far country.
14. P. 172. Annihilated their more civilized brothers.
15. P. 173. Wars between the brothers.
16. P. 179. Hieroglyphical tablets. Cities, highways, pyramids, etc.
17. P. 180. Pyramids like those of Egypt.
18. P. 182. Civilized, tumults of war.
19. P. 183. Cities and roads.
20. P. 184. Savages—annihilated brothers.
21. P. 185. Hieroglyphics.
22. P. 186. Struggles of good and bad.
23. P. 187. Gospel preached in America.
24. P. 188. Destroyed civilization.
25. Pages 189–90. Civilization explained.
26. P. 195. Last civilized people.
27. P. 205. A white and bearded man. Moses (a type of Christ) in Mexico.
28. P. 217. Hebrew writings.
29. Pages 220 & 222. Read plates.
30. P. 223. Buried a book.
31. P. 223. Being a man of letters.
32. P. 224. A book was buried in a hill.
33. P. 225. Book that couldn't be read.
34. Pages 228–29. Isaiah chapter 18. Restoration.
35. P. 230. Restoration.
36. P. 230. "Latter days."
37. P. 231. Restoration. Jeremiah 16:14–16.
38. P. 236. Isaiah's prophecies.
39. P. 247. Stick of Ephraim.
40. P. 249. Received that book.

41. P. 253. The God of Zion is a God of government.
42. Pages 256–57. The mystery of John the Baptist.
43. P. 258. Restored Zion.
44. P. 262. Future restoration.
45. P. 264. Once had a book and were happy.

It is interesting to note that the first edition of *The Book of Mormon* lists Joseph Smith as the author. (He wrote the book to make money, not to start a religion. However, when he found out that people could be deceived so easily into believing his tall tale about the "gold plates," he decided to start his own religion.) Mormons say Joseph Smith listed himself as the author because of the copyright laws. However, the later editions which list Joseph Smith as "translator" were published under the same copyright law.

The Compiler of the Bible

The Mormons have very little respect for the Bible. They do everything in their power to tear it down and attempt to prove it false. One of their arguments along this line concerns the compilation of the Bible. They will ask, "Who compiled the Bible?" They want you to reply that a group of men got together and assembled it. Mormons are taught that the Bible was compiled by men; and because of this, they say, we really cannot trust the Bible. (Those who believe the Bible know that the Holy Spirit is the author of the Bible, using human men whom He inspired. The Holy Spirit compiled the Bible and is preserving it. The Bible was not put together by men.*)

---

* What we today call the Old Testament consists of books commonly recognized by the ancient Jewish people as having come from God. They called it the "word of God," and Jesus Himself so recognized it. It was read publicly and taught regularly in their synagogues. From the very first, Christians accepted these as Holy Scriptures. As the writings of the Apostles appeared

One of the best replies is to ask about the Mormon writings and especially *The Book of Mormon*. Ask them who compiled the material that was supposed to have been on the gold plates that Joseph Smith purportedly got *The Book of Mormon* from. *The Book of Mormon* says very clearly that men compiled it. It also states in a number of places that there were many more plates which had been greatly abridged by many different men. The Bible does not say that any Biblical writings were abridged.

The *Doctrine and Covenants*, section 3, verse 6, says that 116 pages of *The Book of Mormon* are missing because some (e.g., Joseph Smith) "transgressed the commandments and the laws of God, and have gone on in the persuasion of men." One never reads of any part of the Bible being missing as a result of the wickedness of one of the prophets or apostles!

Mormons teach that Joseph Smith only translated one-third of the plates. Thus, two-thirds of the plates have never been translated.

How can Mormons condemn the Bible because of doubts as to how it was compiled? If the reason they give for rejecting the Bible is valid, then a person has even more reason for rejecting *The Book of Mormon*.

they were added to the Jewish Scriptures and held in the same sacred regard. The Council of Carthage, 397 A.D., gave its formal ratification to the 27 books of the New Testament. It did not make the N.T. canon, but merely expressed what had already become the unanimous judgment of the churches— as evidenced by the writings of the Early Church Fathers. (See *Halley's Bible Handbook,* pp. 840–45).

Chapter Twelve

Using *The Book of Mormon* to Witness

As I showed before, *The Book of Mormon* does not contain any of the major Mormon doctrines. But it does contain a lot of material taken out of the King James Bible, often using the same words or just about, without changing the original meaning. Hence one effective means of witnessing and presenting the gospel to Mormons is to use *The Book of Mormon*. I have asked many Mormons to show me LDS doctrine from *The Book of Mormon,* which they cannot do. I have then said, "Let us look at what *The Book of Mormon does* teach." Then I was able to present the following Biblical teachings that are found in *The Book of Mormon* and was able to teach the truth to them from their own book. Referring to *The Book of Mormon* does not mean that you approve of it, but where it correctly quotes the Bible you can use these verses to proclaim the gospel. Also you can show that *The Book of Mormon* does not contain Mormon doctrine in a most positive way.

Since *The Book of Mormon* is so similar to the Bible—because of its many quotes—many people think Mormonism is Christian. However, *The Book of Mormon* is just a bridge to get people from the Bible to the *Doctrine and Covenants*, which contains most of the real Mormon teachings. Most people never read the *Doctrine and Covenants* before they join the Mormon Church so they really do not know what the church teaches. Later on, this is done very subtly.

Joseph Smith once said, ". . . I told the brethren that *The Book of Mormon* was the most correct of any book on earth and the KEYSTONE OF OUR RELIGION, and a man would get nearer to God by abiding by its precepts than by any other book" (*The Teachings of the Prophet Joseph Smith*, p. 194). Most Mormons will agree with that statement. They also will agree with the statement: "As man is, God once was; as God is, man may become." Mormons will usually answer "Yes" to the following questions about God: "Does God have a body with hands, arms, and feet?" "Is He changing—progressing?" "Is there more than one God?"

When a Mormon agrees with these statements, ask if you can show him what *The Book of Mormon* itself teaches concerning this subject and others. (In the quotes below, words that are contrary to Mormon doctrine have been set in italics.)

• • •

1. THERE IS ONLY ONE TRUE GOD, WHO IS ETERNAL. Mormons teach that God the Father, God the Son, and God the Holy Ghost are three distinct gods, that they are not of one essence, and there are many others who have become gods and will do so in the future; none of these has been eternally God.

A. Introduction to *The Book of Mormon*. At the end of the three witnesses's testimony we read, "And the honor be to the Father, and to the Son, and to the Holy Ghost, *which is one God*. Amen."

B. 2 Nephi 11:7, page 80. "For if there be no Christ there be no God, and if there be no God we are not, for there could have been no creation. *But there is a God and he is Christ,* and he cometh in the fullness of his own times."

C. 2 Nephi 26:12, page 101. "And as I spake concerning the convincing of the Jews, that Jesus is the very Christ, it must needs be that the Gentiles be convinced also that *Jesus is the Christ, the Eternal God.*"

D. 2 Nephi 31:21b, page 115. "And now, behold, this is the doctrine of the Father, and of the Son, and of the Holy Ghost, *which is one God,* without end. Amen."

E. Mosiah 7:27a, page 162. "And because he said unto them that *Christ was the God,* the Father of all things. . . ."

F. Mosiah 15:1–5, page 175. "And now Abinadi said unto them: *I would that ye should understand that God himself shall come down among the children of men, and shall redeem his people.* And because he dwelleth in flesh he shall be called the Son of God, and having subjected the flesh to the will of the Father, being the Father and the Son—The Father, because he was conceived by the power of God; and the Son, because of the flesh; thus becoming the Father and Son—*And they are one God,* yea, the very Eternal Father of heaven and of earth. And thus the flesh becoming subject to *the Spirit, or the Son to the Father, being one God,* suffereth temptation, and yieldeth not to the temptation, but suffereth himself to be mocked, and scourged, and cast out, and disowned by his people."

G. Alma 11:22a, 26–29, 38–39 & 44b, pages 235–237.

V. 22a: "And Amulek said unto him: Yea, if it be according to the Spirit of the Lord, which is in me; *for I shall say nothing which is contrary to the Spirit of the Lord.*"

Vv. 26–29: "And Zeezrom said unto him: Thou sayest there is a true and living God? And Amulek said: Yea, there is a true and living God. Now Zeerom said: *Is there more than one God? And he answered, No.*"

Vv. 38–39: "Now Zeezrom saith again unto him: Is the Son of

God the very Eternal Father? And Amulek said unto him: Yea, he is the very Eternal Father of heaven and of earth, and all things which in them are; he is the beginning and the end, the first and the last."

V. 44b: ". . . And shall be brought and be arraigned before the bar of *Christ the Son, and God the Father, and the Holy Spirit, which is one eternal God.*"

• • •

2. GOD IS UNCHANGING. The Mormons teach that God is involved in eternal progression. He is increasing in knowledge and is continuing to change. *The Book of Mormon* does not teach this doctrine, as shown in the following verses.

A. Mormon 9:9–10, & 19, pages 485–86. "*For do we not read that God is the same yesterday, today, and forever, and in him there is no variableness neither shadow of changing?* And now, if ye have imagined up unto yourself a god who doth vary, and in whom there is shadow of changing, then have ye imagined up unto yourselves a god who is not a God of miracles. . . . And if there were miracles wrought then, why has God ceased to be a God of miracles and yet be an unchangeable Being? *And Behold, I say unto you he changeth not;* if so he would cease to be God; and he ceaseth not to be God, and is a God of miracles."

B. Moroni 7:22, page 522. "For behold, *God knowing all things, being from everlasting to everlasting,* behold, he sent angels to minister unto the children of men, to make manifest concerning the coming of Christ; and in Christ there should come every good thing."

C. Moroni 8:18, page 526. "For I know that God is not a partial God, *neither a changeable being; but he is unchangeable from all eternity to all eternity.*"

• • •

3. GOD IS A SPIRIT. Mormons teach that God has a body of flesh and bone and make light of those that believe God is a

spirit as Jesus taught in John 4:24.

A. Alma 18:24–28, page 255. "And Ammon began to speak unto him with boldness, and said unto him: Believest thou that there is a God? And he answered, and said unto him: I do not know what that meaneth. And then Ammon said: *Believest thou that there is a Great Spirit?* And he said, Yea. And Ammon said: This is God. And Ammon said unto him again: *Believest thou that this Great Spirit,* who is God, created all things which are in heaven and in earth?"

B. Alma 22:9–11, page 264. "And the king said: *Is God that Great Spirit* that brought our fathers out of the land of Jerusalem? And Aaron said unto him: *Yea, he is that Great Spirit,* and he created all things both in heaven and in earth. Believest thou this? And he said: Yea, I believe that *the Great Spirit* created all things, and I desire that ye should tell me concerning all these things, and I will believe thy words."

• • •

4. WE ARE TO SEARCH THE SCRIPTURES TO DETERMINE TRUTH. Mormons will tell you to pray about what they are telling you and then you are to receive a warm feeling about what they are telling you, which is to prove it is true. *The Book of Mormon* teaches something different.

Jacob 7:23, page 135. "And it came to pass that peace and the love of God was restored again among the people; and *they searched the scriptures,* and hearkened no more to the words of this wicked man."

• • •

5. THERE IS NO SECOND CHANCE AFTER DEATH. Mormons teach that the LDS gospel will be preached to those in the spirit world after death. These people will then be given another chance to repent and respond to LDS teachings. However, the following verses show that this teaching is false.

A. Mosiah 15:26, page 177. "But behold, and fear, and

tremble before God, for ye ought to tremble; *for the Lord redeemeth none such that rebel against him and die in their sins;* yea, even all those that have perished in their sins ever since the world began, that have willfully rebelled against God, that have known the commandments of God, and would not keep them; these are they that have no part in the first resurrection."

B. Alma 34:33–35, page 295. "And now, as I said unto you before, as ye have had so many witnesses, therefore, *I beseech of you that ye do not procrastinate the day of your repentance until the end; for after this day of life, which is given us to prepare for eternity, behold, if we do not improve our time while in this life, then cometh the night of darkness wherein there can be no labor performed.* Ye cannot say, when ye are brought to that awful crisis, that I will repent, that I will return to my God. Nay, ye cannot say this; for that same spirit which doth possess your bodies at the time that ye go out of this life, will have power to possess your body in that eternal world. *For behold, if ye have procrastinated the day of your repentance even unto death, behold, ye have become subjected to the spirit of the devil, and he doth seal you his; therefore, the Spirit of the Lord hath withdrawn from you, and hath no place in you, and the devil hath all power over you; and this is the final state of the wicked.*

· · ·

6. THE AUTHORITY TO BAPTIZE COMES FROM JESUS CHRIST, NOT FROM JOHN THE BAPTIST LIKE THE MORMON CHURCH TEACHES.

3 Nephi 11:25, page 429. "*Having authority given me of Jesus Christ, I baptize* you in the name of the Father, and of the Son, and of the Holy Ghost. Amen."

· · ·

7. REVELATION COMES THROUGH THE HOLY SPIRIT, NOT BY ANGELS OR OTHER PEOPLE.

Alma 5:46, page 221. "*Behold, I say unto you they are made known unto me by the Holy Spirit of God.* Behold, I have fasted and prayed many days that I might know these things of myself. *And now I do know of myself that they are true; for the Lord God hath made them manifest unto me by his Holy Spirit: and this is the spirit of revelation which is in me."*

Proclaim the Way of Salvation

Your purpose in communication with Mormons is to help them realize that we are all unholy sinners before God, have all willfully sinned, are dead in the trespasses of sin and unable to do *anything* to save ourselves or help us merit salvation. *Jesus only saves sinners,* so it is first necessary for a person to realize his sinful nature before he will recognize his need for accepting Jesus Christ as his personal Savior. There are some passages in *The Book of Mormon* that you can use to present this truth. A few of them are:

1. Mosiah 16:15, page 179. "Teach them that redemption cometh through Christ the Lord, who is the very Eternal Father. Amen."

2. Mosiah 3:18, page 153. ". . . salvation was, and is, and is to come, in and through the atoning blood of Christ, the Lord Omnipotent."

3. Alma 5:14, page 218. "And now behold, I ask of you, my brethren of the church, have ye spiritually been born of God? Have ye received his image in your countenance? Have ye experienced this mighty change in your hearts?"

4. Mosiah 27:24–28, page 201. (This is a passage which is very difficult for Mormons to deal with. It is very obvious that it is a comment on John 3. It presents the true way of salvation and walks all over Mormon doctrine, as I have indicated by the use of italics.) "24. For, said he, *I have repented of my sins, and have been redeemed of the Lord;* behold *I am* born of the Spirit. 25. And the Lord said unto me: Marvel not that all mankind, yea, men and women, all nations, kindreds, tongues and people, *must be born again;* yea, *born of God, changed from their carnal and fallen state,*

to a state of righteousness, being redeemed of God, becoming his sons and daughters; 26. And thus they *become* new creatures; and unless they do this, they can in nowise inherit the kingdom of God. 27. I say unto you, unless this be the case, they *must be cast off;* and this I know, because I was like to be cast off. 28. Nevertheless, after wading through much tribulation, repenting nigh unto death, the Lord in mercy hath seen fit *to snatch me out of the everlasting burning, and I am born of God.*"

Go through these verses very slowly. Do not let the missionaries get by with glib answers or false statements. Here, for example, are some of the questions you can ask. (You will note that I often speak about the "blood" of Jesus Christ. Mormons do not like the blood. Christians know there is "power in the blood," so speak often about the blood of Christ which was shed upon the cross for our sins.)

(1) "Can you say that you have repented of every one of your own personal sins?"

(2) "Redeemed" (v. 24) is an interesting word. It means "to buy back," "to obtain the release or restoration of, as from captivity, by paying a ransom." John 8:44 states that by nature we are children of the devil. Acts 26:18 informs us that we are under the power of Satan. Thus it is from Satan and his power that we need to be redeemed. Mosiah 16:15 in *The Book of Mormon* declares ". . . that redemption cometh through Christ the Lord." Question: "You will note that this statement in Mosiah 27:24 is in the past tense. Can *you* say that you *have been* redeemed 100% by and only by the blood of Jesus Christ and are absolutely sure that you will go to the celestial kingdom immediately when you die?"

(3) "'Behold I am born of the Spirit.' I understand that the LDS Church teaches that being "born again" is a long process, but this verse says that we can be sure of it right now. Can you say that you have been born of God through the blood of Jesus?"

If either of them says "Yes," ask him to describe how it happened and listen carefully to what he has to say. (I have had Mormons say to me that they *were* born again, even though they knew they weren't—just to deceive me. When I questioned them, however, they had to back down.)

(4) V. 25. "Note again the necessity of being born again and that this is something that only God can do—and it is possible because of the blood Jesus shed on the cross for our sins. Do you claim that your standing before God is a work that *He* has done in your life and it has nothing to do with what *you* have done or your relationship to the LDS Church?"

(5) "'Changed from their carnal and fallen state.' This strikes me as a very amazing statement to be found in *The Book of Mormon*. I understand that the LDS Church does not believe in 'original sin.'" (In the book *Mormon Doctrine,* written by Bruce R. McConkie, he states on page 550 under the heading ORIGINAL SIN THEORY that it is a 'false doctrine.' In another standard work of the Mormon Church, *Doctrine and Covenants,* Section 29, verses 46–50, it states that children "cannot sin" because they are born pure and innocent. In *The Book of Mormon*, Moroni 8:8, on page 525, we read: ". . . little children are whole, for they are not capable of committing sin. . . .") "Would you tell me how a person could be saved from 'their carnal and fallen state' if they were never *in* such a state? Thus *The Book of Mormon* and the LDS Church teach two conflicting things. Which is correct?"

(6) "What does it mean to be in 'a state of righteousness'? If it depends upon a person's 'worthiness,' how could they ever have the complete assurance of being in 'a state of righteousness' before God?"

(7) "'Becoming his sons and daughters.' I understand that you Mormons teach that people have *always* been 'sons and daughters' of God because of your claim that each person had a 'preexistence.' If we were always 'sons and daughters,' then why does

this passage state that it is something that one *becomes* because he has been *redeemed* from his sins through the precious blood of Christ and has come into 'a state of righteousness'? This is very puzzling. Would you please explain this to me?"

(8) V. 27. "'. . . they must be cast off.' To me, this says that it is possible for people to go into the 'second death' because they refuse to repent and turn to Christ to redeem them from their many personal sins. I thought that only murderers who refuse to shed their own blood, and excommunicated Mormons, were the ones who go into the 'second death.' Could you clear up this confusion for me?"

(9) V. 28. "'. . . snatch me out of the everlasting burning.' This statement would seem to go along with the Biblical view that man by nature is in a 'carnal and fallen state' and unless a person is born of God through the redemption made possible through the blood of Jesus that he or she will end up in 'everlasting burning' which is the 'second death.' Would this conclusion be correct?" (If they say "Yes," it would be admitting that Mormon doctrine on this subject is not the truth; and if they say "No," they are in conflict with what is written here.)

(10) "'I am born of God.' Do you have this kind of assurance—that you have been saved from your carnal and fallen state, are completely righteous before God, and 100% certain of going to the celestial kingdom the very moment you die?"

Book of Mormon Quotations from the Bible

There is yet another way you can show that *The Book of Mormon* is not inspired of God and didn't originate on gold plates. Joseph Smith claimed he translated *The Book of Mormon* from gold plates that were written in "Reformed Egyptian"; but while reading *The Book of Mormon* I recognized that large portions were taken *directly* from the sixth edition of the King James Bible that was being used in the days of Joseph Smith. Many chapters are copied almost word for word from the King James Bible. For instance, in 1 Nephi 20 to 21 (on pages 46–50), Isaiah 48 and 49 are quoted. In 2 Nephi 12 to 24 (on pages 81–96), Isaiah 2 through 14 is quoted. Then in Mosiah 14 (pages 174–5), Isaiah 53 is quoted. Also portions of many other verses from the King James Bible are used in *The Book of Mormon*.

Many of these quotes from the King James Bible found in *The Book of Mormon* are taken from the New Testament, which, as everyone knows, was written in A.D.; but in *The Book of Mormon* these New Testament quotes are placed in what is there dated as B.C.! Furthermore, if scholars translated accurately, it would be impossible to translate a passage from the Hebrew or the Greek and another from Reformed Egyptian and come out with identical wordings. You could have the same *meaning* but not the same *wording*. Here is an analogy found in the Bible itself: There are some Old Testament verses quoted in the New Testament which read differently from what was originally written in the Old Testament. Why is this so? Because these quotes have been taken from the Septuagint, which is the Old Testament translated into Greek. One example of this is in 1 Peter 1:24, where Peter quotes Isaiah 40:6–8. (Notice the differences in wording.)

Many of the key characters in *The Book of Mormon* are taken from the Bible with just different names, and with a few of the details changed. Furthermore, Joseph Smith quoted from some of the books of the Apocrypha, and the King James Bible that Joseph Smith used included the Apocrypha.

In 2 Nephi 22:2 (page 93) there is clear proof that Joseph Smith plagiarized from the King James Bible when he wrote *The Book of Mormon*. In this chapter, Joseph Smith is quoting from Isaiah chapter 12. The word "Jehovah" is used only four times in the King James Bible. Isaiah 12:2 is one of those places. In the KJV the word Jehovah is printed in bold capitals (**JEHOVAH**) in these four places. Is it just a coincidence that in *The Book of*

Mormon, in 2 Nephi 22:2, the word Jehovah is also found in bold capitals *exactly* as in Isaiah 12:2? Remember, Joseph Smith claimed that God gave him the translation. However, Jehovah is a *false* rendering for the name of God—a word that was made up in the 12th century. Most scholars today would agree that God's name in Hebrew is "Yahweh." Surely God would have known how to pronounce His own name! (It is good to let your Mormon friends see these two places with their own eyes, if you have a King James Bible.)

Why Were the Gold Plates Not Inscribed in Hebrew?

One further problem: Joseph Smith claimed that the gold plates from which he supposedly translated *The Book of Mormon* were written in "Reformed Egyptian." This fact is very strange indeed! Remember, the people written about in *The Book of Mormon* are supposed to be Hebrews. All of the Old Testament was written in Hebrew, with the exception of a few verses written in Aramaic. The twelve tribes departed from Egypt in about 1490 B.C., but *The Book of Mormon* starts in 600 B.C. So these Israelites had been out of Egypt for over eight hundred years. Furthermore, *The Book of Mormon* covers a period of over 1000 years, ending in 421 A.D. Why would any of these people in AMERICA still be speaking Egyptian and know it well enough to write in that difficult script? From evidence contained in *The Book of Mormon* (Mormon 9:33), these Israelite-Amerindians still spoke Hebrew. So why would they be recording their history in Reformed Egyptian during these many centuries?

A flimsy explanation—purportedly offered by several scribes and recorded within *The Book of Mormon* text—is that space was limited on the gold plates, which is why the authors wrote not in Hebrew but in Reformed Egyptian. But did all the writing need to be crammed onto one or just a few plates? No! During the many centuries that these men were presumably recording their national history, surely additional blank plates could have been manufactured—for these Nephites and Lamanites were not primitive nomads. Theirs was a great civilization, if you believe the story! The supposed reason for these national archives being written in a "foreign" language rather than Hebrew is far from convincing.

Equally strange is this conspicuous fact: The 15 separate books that comprise *The Book of Mormon*—supposedly engraved on these gold plates by 14 ancient authors and spanning 1000 years—from First Nephi through Moroni, are stylistically identical! Monotonously so. Unlike the Bible—God's matchless, inspired Word—there is an obvious sameness throughout the whole. Very strange!

The favorite expression of these 14 scribes, occurring 1272 times in all, is "It came to pass." This, along with "Yea, behold," "And behold," "But behold"—the repetition is astounding—produce a distinctly King James flavor. How could this have happened? Very strange indeed!

Chapter Thirteen

Scriptures Misapplied

EVEN though Mormons try to undermine the authority of the Bible every chance they get, they use it in an effort to try to prove their teachings. Often when they approach a person, they will make their initial appeal from the Bible and not from *The Book of Mormon*. This is the first step in their indoctrination process. The whole Mormon system is in direct contradiction to the Bible (in spite of the fact that they call their doctrines the "restored" gospel). However, if they admitted this from the beginning, most people would not want to listen to them. For this reason, they use Bible verses taken out of context and present their teachings as "Christianity plus." While rejecting the truth of the Bible, they use it to try to "prove" their teachings. At the same time, they try to disprove the doctrines of Christianity which are based 100% upon the Bible.

When I started witnessing to Mormons I used many scripture passages in order to prove them wrong. However, I found that this was not very effective. I knew I needed to change my approach, so I spent much time in thought and prayer. I decided to take the verses that *they* were quoting and show them that these verses did *not* prove their point. I was able to do this because they were taking verses out of context or were otherwise completely missing the point of the verse. I found that *this method is very effective.* For this reason, I have listed most of the verses they misuse and will show you how to utilize them.

Are There Multiple Gods?

John 10:34—"Jesus answered them, Is it not written in your law, I said, Ye are gods?" This verse, along with 1 Corinthians 8:5, is used to try to prove their teaching that men can become gods in the future and have their own worlds. They point to the word "gods" and get so excited that they completely ignore what the verse actually says. When they use this verse, my conversation goes as follows:

Q. Would you mind reading the verse to me again?

A. I would be glad to. (They read the verse.)

Q. You understand English, don't you?

A. Of course I do.

Q. I think you will agree that "are" is a verb in the present tense.

A. Yes, that's right.

Q. Are you "a god" right now?

A. Of course not. We don't believe that you can be "a god" right now. That pertains to the future.

Q. Just a minute. You're the one who brought up this verse. It's clearly in the present tense. When I asked if you were "a god" right now, you answered "No." What kind of exegesis is this? You take a verse that is plainly speaking about a present situation and apply it to the future. Is this a typical example of your teaching?

A. (Silence.)

What, then, is the correct interpretation of Jesus' words? John 10:34 quotes Psalm 82:6. When you look at the context—the whole psalm—and especially at verse 7, you can see that it is in the present tense and talking about "judges" here upon this earth. Psalm 82:6–7 says, "I have said, Ye are gods; and all of you are children of the Most High. But ye shall die like men, and fall like one of the princes." Only the warning relates to the future.

Is There a Third Testament?

Ezekiel 37:15–22—This passage talks about the stick of Judah and the stick of Ephraim. Mormons like to use this reference to try to prove that *The Book of Mormon* was inspired by God. However, they hope you will read only verses 15 to 20. They will point out that, in Old Testament times, books were not in codex form but were scrolls, made of parchment wrapped around sticks. They will tell you that these two sticks represent two sacred writings that are to be joined together. Supposedly, the "stick of Judah" is the Bible and the "stick of Ephraim" is *The Book of Mormon*, and these two volumes should be considered as one book. They imply that *The Book of Mormon* is of equal inspiration with the Bible. (In reality, they believe *The Book of Mormon* is far more inspired than the Bible.) They claim that the Bible was written for people living in the Holy Land and Europe and *The Book of Mormon* was written for inhabitants of the Western Hemisphere. On the cover the latter is the statement: "Another Testament of Jesus Christ."

What a strained interpretation! Ezekiel 37:15–22 is talking about two nations which will no longer be two, but one. This prophecy speaks of the reuniting of the Northern Kingdom (represented by Ephraim) and the Southern Kingdom (represented by Judah). This can be clearly seen if the whole passage is read in context.

The Hebrew word for "stick" is used in only one other place in the Bible—2 Kings 6:6. "And the man of God said, Where fell it? And he shewed him the place. And he cut down a stick, and cast it thither, and the iron did swim." The same Hebrew word is used here as in Ezekiel. Ezekiel was familiar with the word "scroll," and made reference to it at least four times in his writings. Notice

Ezekiel 2:9 where "roll of a book" is a reference to a scroll and Ezekiel 3:1–3 where "roll" refers to a scroll.

These verses in Ezekiel 37 about the "stick of Ephraim" have nothing to do with *The Book of Mormon*. This can even be proved from *The Book of Mormon,* where Alma 10:3 says: "And Aminadi was a descendant of Nephi, who was the son of Lehi, who came out of the land of Jerusalem, who was a descendant of *Manasseh,* who was the son of Joseph who was sold into Egypt by the hand of his brethren." The people who are supposed to have written *The Book of Mormon* were descendants of Manasseh and not Ephraim, again showing that the Ezekiel passage fails to prove that *The Book of Mormon* is true.

Another thing Mormons conveniently ignore is that *The Book of Mormon* was never in the form of a scroll (as their story goes), but on plates wired together in the form of a book.

Did Isaiah Predict *The Book of Mormon*?

Isaiah 29:1–14—From this passage, Mormons mainly use verses 11 and 12: "And the vision of all is become unto you as the words of a book that is sealed, which men deliver to one that is learned, saying, Read this, I pray thee: and he saith, I cannot; for it is sealed. And the book is delivered to him that is not learned, saying, Read this, I pray thee: and he saith, I am not learned."

Mormons infer that the sealed book spoken of in this prophecy is *The Book of Mormon*. However, a close examination of both the Bible and the Mormons' own story shows their contention to be false.

The Mormons' story goes as follows (found in the *Times and Seasons*, Vol. 3, p. 773). Martin Harris says: "I went to the city of New York and presented the characters [those purported to have been on the gold plates that were the source of *The Book of Mormon*] which had been translated, with the translation thereof to Professor Anthon, a gentleman celebrated for his literary attainments:—Professor Anthon stated that the translation was correct, more so than any he had before seen translated from the Egyptian. I then showed him those which were not yet translated, and he said that they were Egyptian, Chaldean, Assyrian, and Arabian, and he said that they were the true characters. He gave me a certificate certifying to the people of Palmyra that they were true characters, and that the translation of such of them as had been translated was also correct. I took the certificate and put it into my pocket, and was just leaving the house, when Mr. Anthon called me back, and asked me how the young man found out that there were gold plates in the place where he found them. I answered that an angel of God had revealed it unto him.

"He then said to me, 'Let me see that certificate.' I accordingly took it out of my pocket and gave it to him, when he took it and tore it to pieces, saying that there was no such thing now as ministering of angels, and that if I would bring the plates to him, he would translate them. I informed him that part of the plates were sealed, and that I was forbidden to bring them; he replied, 'I cannot read a sealed book.' I left him and went to Dr. Mitchel who sanctioned what Professor Anthon had said respecting both the characters and the translation."

The Mormons say that the words of Professor Anthon, "I cannot read a sealed book" are a fulfillment of this Isaiah passage. However, what they are teaching can be disproved.

First, Professor Anthon denies the story in a written statement. He said: "The whole story about my pronouncing the Mormon inscription to be reformed Egyptian hieroglyphics is perfectly false. Some years ago, a plain, apparently simple-hearted farmer called on me with the note from Dr. Mitchel, of our city, now dead, requesting me to decipher, if possible, the paper which the farmer would hand me. Upon examining the paper in question, I soon came to the conclusion that it was all a trick—perhaps a hoax. . . . I have frequently conversed with friends on the subject since the

Mormon excitement began and well remember that the paper contained anything else but Egyptian hieroglyphics."

Second, *The Book of Mormon* itself makes the whole story impossible. It says:

> And now, behold, we have written this record according to our knowledge in the characters which are called among us the reformed Egyptian, being handed down and altered by us, according to our manner of speech. And if our plates had been sufficiently large we would have written in Hebrew: but the Hebrew hath been altered by us also; and if we could have written in Hebrew, behold, ye would have had no imperfection in our record. But the Lord knoweth the things we have written and also that none other people knoweth our language; therefore he hath prepared means for the interpretation thereof (Mormon 9:32–34).

This passage states that the reformed Egyptian that was on the gold plates had been altered and "none other people knoweth our language." It was impossible for anyone else to read it. Since there is no trace of reformed Egyptian found in the Americas and only the Egyptian language of Egypt can be studied, it was impossible for Professor Anthon to have read the characters as Martin Harris stated. The book they are trying to prove shows that the story is false.

Third, the true meaning of the Isaiah passage can be determined. Isaiah 29:9–12 is not talking about a "sealed book." Verse 11 says, "as the words of a book that is sealed." The word "as" is very important. This passage says that God has clearly revealed His Word to the people, but because of the sinfulness and hardness of their hearts, they do not understand the words. Even today, those who live in sin and disobedience to God cannot understand the Bible. However, what was once a sealed book can become an open book when one desires to know the truth. Many Christians can testify to this, because before they came to know

Jesus Christ as their own personal Savior they did not understand the Bible. They could read the words, but the words meant nothing to them. Once they were saved and the Holy Spirit dwelt in their hearts, they were able to read the Bible and understand what it says.

Did Jeremiah Foresee *The Book of Mormon*?

Jeremiah 36:2—"Take thee a roll [scroll] of a book and write therein all the words that I have spoken unto thee against Israel. . . ." Mormons use this passage to show that people wrote on scrolls in Old Testament times and then use it in connection with the Ezekiel 37:15–22 passage which has already been discussed. However, the Mormons teach that *The Book of Mormon* was written on gold plates and not a scroll. How can they use the two sticks to represent the Bible and *The Book of Mormon* when *The Book of Mormon* was written on gold plates?

Who Are Jesus' "Other Sheep"?

John 10:16—"And other sheep I have, that are not of this fold; them also I must bring, and they shall hear my voice; and there shall be one fold, and one shepherd." Mormons interpret this passage as a prophecy to try to prove *The Book of Mormon*. They say that the phrase "other sheep" applies to the people that *The Book of Mormon* says came to America. They refer you to Jesus' statement in Matthew 15:24: "But he answered and said, I am not sent but unto the lost sheep of the house of Israel." From this they conclude the "other sheep" could not be Gentiles.

However, a quick survey of other scriptures shows that John 10:16 does apply to the Gentiles and has nothing to do with *The Book of Mormon*. Isaiah 56:8 states, "The Lord God, which gathereth the outcasts of Israel, saith, Yet will I gather others to him, beside those that are gathered unto him." John 17:20 says,

"Neither pray I for these alone, but for them also which shall believe on me through their word." Now read Acts 15:7–9 and Ephesians 2:11–19: Gentiles were being gathered in. The "other sheep" are people who were not Jews, and this verse in no way proves *The Book of Mormon*.

Did Elijah Commission Joseph Smith?

Malachi 4:5–6—Mormons teach that on April 3, 1836, Elijah appeared to Joseph Smith and at that time gave him the "keys of the dispensation for the turning of the hearts of the fathers to the children, and the hearts of the children to their fathers." They use this passage, along with 1 Corinthians 15:29, to support their doctrine of baptism for the dead.

However, in Matthew 11:10–14 Jesus clearly explained what this passage in Malachi means. Verse 14 passages reads, "And if ye will receive it, this is Elias [ie., Elijah], which was to come." This refers to the passage in Malachi, and shows that the fulfillment was in John the Baptist. The subject is also covered in Matthew 17:11–13: "And Jesus answered and said unto them, Elias truly shall first come, and restore all things. But I say unto you, That Elias is come already, and they knew him not, but have done unto him whatsoever they listed. Likewise shall also the Son of man suffer of them. Then the disciples understood that he spoke unto them of John the Baptist." These verses indicate that Malachi 4:5–6 was fulfilled in John the Baptist. Note that Jesus said, "That Elias is come already." The Malachi passage had already been fulfilled in Jesus' day. Another reference to Elias in Luke 1:17 supports the same conclusion.

And what is the correct interpretation of 1 Corinthians 15:29—the only mention in Scripture of anyone being "baptized for the dead"? Look at the verse itself: "Else what shall they do which are baptized for the dead, if the dead rise not at all? Why are they then baptized for the dead?"

Note carefully what is said here. It is clear from the context that Paul distinguished his own practice from that described here. He merely held up the teaching of being "baptized for the dead" as a practice of some who denied the resurrection of the dead.

How the false teachers came to this view may never be known, but just north of Corinth lay Eleusis, the center of an ancient mystery religion, whose rites of initiation were washings of purification in the sea. Given the Corinthian propensity for distortion in matters of church practice (11:2–14:40) it is likely that some in Corinth were propounding a false view of baptism which Paul took up and used as an argument against people who denied the Resurrection. He does not sanction or recommend the practice!

Do Mormons Preach the Everlasting Gospel?

Revelation 14:6—Mormons apply this phrase "everlasting gospel" to their beliefs alone. They say that the gospel was lost through a "complete falling away" and that it was restored via Joseph Smith. They assert that they, and they alone, are the ones who are commissioned to preach it to the world.

1 Corinthians 15:1–5 provides a clear description of the gospel—the good news based on the death and resurrection of Jesus Christ. There are over 100 references to the gospel in the New Testament. In all Biblical references to the gospel, the emphasized fact is the death and resurrection of Jesus Christ: that Christ died for our sins, and that he rose again for our justification. (It is well worth your time and effort to find all the references to the gospel by using an exhaustive concordance.)

Mormons claim that water baptism is part of the gospel. But in 1 Corinthians 1:17, Paul writes: "For Christ sent me not to baptize, but to preach the gospel; not with wisdom of words, lest the cross of Christ should be made of none effect." Water baptism plays no part in our eternal salvation but identifies us with Christ after we have been born again.

Are "Spiritual Feelings" Reliable?

1 Corinthians 2:9–13—"But as it is written, Eye hath not seen, nor ear heard, neither have entered into the heart of man, the things which God hath prepared for them that love him. But God hath revealed them unto us by his Spirit: for the Spirit searcheth all things, yea, the deep things of God. For what man knoweth the things of man, save the spirit of man which is in him? Even so the things of God knoweth no man, but the Spirit of God. Now we have received, not the spirit of the world, but the Spirit which is of God; that we might know the things that are freely given to us of God. Which things also we speak, not in the words which man's wisdom teacheth, but which the Holy Ghost teacheth; comparing spiritual things with spiritual."

Mormons have twisted this passage beyond recognition. They teach that the way to test the trustworthiness of a teaching or person is by the Spirit and prayer. The problem is that Mormons take this to mean an absolute reliance on feelings. To a Mormon, feelings become far more important than facts. When you try to show Mormons the facts, they don't want to look at them. They will question every source you use. Sometimes they don't even care what their *own* books say! All that matters is that they feel that they are right.

However, the Bible tells us how we are to test religions. One good verse is Deuteronomy 13:14, which says that when the truth of a disputed statement is to be ascertained (note the context, verses 12–15), "Then shalt thou inquire, and make search, and ask diligently; and behold, if it be truth, and the thing certain, that such abomination is wrought among you. . . ." The Mormons must be forced to consider what it means to "inquire," to "make search," to "ask diligently," and how this differs from mere feelings. The Bible requires tests based on Biblical truth.

Another important verse is Acts 17:11: "These were more noble than those in Thessalonica, in that they received the word with all readiness of mind, and searched the scriptures daily, whether those things were so." Paul had come to the Berean people and was preaching a new doctrine. Before they would receive it, they searched the Bible to make sure that what Paul said was true. These people did not test it by a good feeling or by empty prayers. They checked out the facts. This is the way all religions must be tested. The writers of the New Testament constantly appealed to Scripture to prove their points. In Matthew and Hebrews alone there are over 200 quotes from the Old Testament.

How would Mormons answer the many religious groups like the Community of Christ (formerly the Reorganized Church of Jesus Christ of Latter-day Saints), Muslims,* Roman Catholics, Children of God, Unification Church, Jehovah Witnesses, etc.? They all have prophets, claim to receive revelations from God, have extra-Biblical writings, are similar in organization, and say they are the only true church. It is obvious that this cannot be true. How then is a person to know which group is right? It is only after deep study of the teachings of each group in comparison with Biblical statements that one can tell if these groups offer the truth. Feelings can easily deceive a person. Many people's feelings tell them they are in love, and on these feelings alone they get married. After a couple marries and gets to know each other, they find that their feelings really didn't add up to love; the feelings disappear, and what was thought to be true and lasting love ends in divorce. Neither love nor religion should be based on feelings.

In general, feelings are important for Mormons because the Mormon church discourages investigation of the truth. Often they will not tell the truth about what they believe even if they are asked point-blank about their beliefs. They will not admit that while it is easy to get into the Mormon church, it is difficult to get out. The only way a person can get out is to be excommu-

---

* See Appendix for parallels between Mormonism and Islam.

nicated. If Mormons really had the truth, they would be happy to have inquirers delve deeply into their religion before joining the church. However, since a person would not become a Mormon if he knew the truth, the LDS Church tries to use these verses to keep prospects from investigating their beliefs.

Who or What Is the "Rock"?

Matthew 16:13–19—"When Jesus came into the coast of Caesarea Philippi, he asked his disciples, saying, Whom do men say that I the Son of man am? And they said, Some say that thou art John the Baptist; some, Elias; and others, Jeremias, or one of the prophets. He saith unto them, But whom say ye that I am? And Simon Peter answered and said, Thou art the Christ, the Son of the living God. And Jesus answered and said unto him, Blessed art thou, Simon Bar-jona; for flesh and blood hath not revealed it unto thee, but my Father which is in heaven. And I say also unto thee, That thou art Peter, and upon this rock I will build my church; and the gates of hell shall not prevail against it. And I will give unto thee the keys of the kingdom of heaven: and whatsoever thou shalt bind on earth shall be bound in heaven: and whatsoever thou shalt loose on earth shall be loosed in heaven."

Mormons misinterpret this passage in two ways.

The first involves the word "rock" in verse 18. They view this as the "rock of revelation" and argue that it proves the need for new revelations. They say the new "revelation" is "Thou are the Christ, the Son of the living God." Mormons give more attention to the idea of a new revelation than to Christ himself. A careful study of the word "rock" in the Bible shows that the rock is Christ and not revelation. The following verses support this conclusion.

Exodus 17:6 says, "Behold, I will stand before thee there upon the rock in Horeb; and thou shalt smite the rock, and there shall come water out of it, that the people may drink. And Moses did so in the sight of the elders of Israel." This verse provides the background for two New Testament passages which make it clear that the Lord himself is the rock.

John 7:37–38 says, "In the last day, that great day of the feast, Jesus stood and cried, saying, If any man thirst, let him come unto me, and drink. He that believeth on me, as the scripture hath said, out of his belly [i.e., heart] shall flow rivers of living water." 1 Corinthians 10:4 says, "And did all drink the same spiritual drink: for they drank of that spiritual Rock that followed them, and that Rock was Christ." It is obvious that the rock is Christ. The church is built upon Christ and not on new revelation. (See also Deut. 32:3–4, 15, 30–31; 2 Sam. 23:2–3; Ps. 62:2; 118:22; Acts 4:10–12; Rom. 9:32–33; and 1 Pet. 2:4, 6–8.)

The second error in Mormon teaching on Matthew 16:13–19 is that they say that Peter was the head of the church. In this respect they, along with many others, resemble the Roman Catholic Church. The Mormons make a great mistake in not knowing what the Bible really says on this subject. Actually James, Jesus' half-brother (not to be confused with the Apostle James), was more respected than Peter. (See Acts 12:17; 15:13; 21:18; Gal. 2:11–12 for examples of James' primacy.)

Does God Have Body Parts?

Exodus 24:10—"And they saw the God of Israel: and there was under his feet as it were a paved work of a sapphire stone, and as it were the body of heaven in his clearness." Using this verse and other verses, the Mormons argue that the Bible is in harmony with their doctrine that "God has a body of flesh and bone." However, the real basis for their belief that God has a body is the revised testimony of Joseph Smith, in which he stated that in 1820 he actually *saw* God! Smith declared, "It no sooner appeared than I found myself delivered from the enemy which held me bound. When the light rested upon me I saw two personages, whose brightness and glory defy all description, standing above me in the air. One of them spoke unto me, calling me by name, and said, pointing to the other—'This is My Beloved Son. Hear Him!'" This is the story as told by Mormons *today*, and most Mormons believe that it is true. There are two ways to answer this assertion. One is from Mormon writings, and the other is from the Bible.

One day, while talking with two Mormon missionaries, I quoted a number of passages showing that God was invisible and that no one had ever seen God. (See John 1:18; Colossians 1:15; 1 Timothy 1:17; 6:16; 1 John 4:12.) As I read these verses, the missionaries said they were in agreement with me. But then they said, "But what if you actually saw God?"—as if it did not make any difference what the Bible said. The alleged experience of Joseph Smith was more important. They felt that God's appearance to Joseph Smith was an unquestionable fact. However, it was not until 1842 (twelve years after the founding of the Mormon Church), that the *present* "first-written" account appeared saying that Joseph Smith actually saw *God*. In recent years, there have been a number of accounts that have turned up showing clearly that for many years the LDS Church taught that Joseph Smith saw only the *Lord* (the Son), an angel, or angels.

One of the earliest accounts of the First Vision is in Joseph Smith's handwriting and is dated about 1833. It reads as follows:

> The Lord heard my cry in the wilderness and while in the attitude of calling upon the Lord in the 16th year of my age a pillar of light above the brightness of the sun at noon day came down from above and rested upon me and I was filled with the Spirit of God and the Lord opened the heavens upon me and I saw the Lord and he spoke unto me saying, "Joseph my son, thy sins are forgiven thee. Go thy way, walk in my statutes and keep my commandments; behold I am the Lord of glory. I was crucified for the world that all those who believe on my name may

have eternal life. . . ." (*Brigham Young University Studies*, Spring 1969, page 281).

There is no reference here to seeing God the Father. Another handwritten account, from 1835, reads as follows:

> November 1835. . . . I called on the Lord in mighty prayer. A pillar of fire appeared above my head; which presently rested down upon me, and filled me with unspeakable joy. A personage appeared in the midst of this pillar of flame, which was spread all around and yet nothing consumed. Another personage soon appeared like unto the first; he said unto me, "Thy sins are forgiven thee." He testified also unto me that Jesus Christ is the Son of God. I saw many angels in the vision. I was about 14 years old when I received this first communication.

Two of the presidents of the Mormon church state that *only* an angel appeared to Joseph Smith. The first is Brigham Young in the *Journal of Discourses*, Vol. 2, page 171: "The Lord did not come with the armies of heaven, in power and great glory, nor send His messengers panoplied with aught else than the truth of heaven, to communicate to the meek, the lowly, the youth of humble origin, the sincere inquirer after the knowledge of God. But He did send His angel to this same obscure person, Joseph Smith jun.[sic], who afterwards became a Prophet, Seer, and Revelator, and informed him that he should not join any of the religious sects of the day, for they were all wrong; that they were following the precepts of men instead of the Lord Jesus. . . ." There can be no question that Brigham Young was talking about the First Vision. So note that he says, "The Lord did not come. . . . But He did send His angel." If Joseph Smith saw *God* as he claims, this would have been the greatest revelation given to any man that ever lived! It would surpass anything revealed in the Bible. A truthful person could not be in error repeatedly about something that was so momentous. Yet Brigham Young here, Joseph Smith in 1835, and others speak only of an angel or angels. How this undermines Smith's revised testimony of 1842!

A second Mormon church president, John Taylor, explains in the *Journal of Discourses*, Vol. 10, page 127: "How did this state of things called Mormonism originate? We read that an angel came down and revealed himself to Joseph Smith and manifested unto him in a vision the true position of the world in a religious point of view. He was surrounded with light and glory while the heavenly messenger communicated these things unto him. . . ." (Many similar quotations are found in the booklet *Where Does It Say That?*)

Mormons use the following logic and scriptures to try to prove that God has a body of flesh and bone:

Exodus 24:10: "And they saw the God of Israel: and there was under his feet as it were a paved work of a sapphire stone, and as it were the body of heaven in his clearness." They point out the words, "And they saw the God of Israel," and feel that they have proved that God has a body. According to Mormon teachings, "the God of Israel" was the Lord Jesus Christ, who they say was the Jehovah of the Old Testament. In order to be consistent with their own teachings, they have to admit that this verse is talking about Jehovah, who is the Son, not the Father. However, they also teach that Jesus did not possess a body until he was born into this world! They believe, likewise, that one must have a body in order to become a god! How could Jehovah (Jesus Christ), be God in the Old Testament without having an earthly body so that he could progress and become God? (You won't get much of an answer to this question.)

The Mormons try to prove their teaching that God has a physical body by using passages of Scripture which talk about God having body parts. For example, Exodus 19:9 says, "And the Lord said unto Moses, Lo, I come unto thee in a thick cloud, that the people may hear when I speak with thee, and believe thee for ever." Mormons argue that God must have a literal mouth to be able to speak. Psalm 94:7–11 reads: ". . . The Lord shall not see, neither shall the God of Jacob regard it. Understand, ye brutish among the people: and ye fools, when will ye be wise? He that planted the ear, shall he not hear? He that formed the eye, shall he not see? He that chastiseth the heathen, shall not he correct? He that teacheth man knowledge, shall not he know? The Lord knoweth the thoughts of man, that they are vanity." Mormons maintain that God has to have eyes or he would not be able to see! Genesis 8:21: "And the Lord smelled a sweet savour. . . ." Again they say God has to have a nose or he would not be able to smell!

There are several ways to answer this argument. "Do you believe God has feathers and wings?" I point out that logic like the above will force us to that conclusion. I say: "Psalm 91:4 says, 'He shall cover thee with his feathers, and under his wings shall thou trust: his truth shall be thy shield and buckler.' Does this mean that God has the constitution of a bird? Isaiah 19:1 says: 'Behold, the Lord rideth upon a swift cloud, and shall come into Egypt. . . .' I have never seen a man ride on the clouds without wings. Exodus 31:18 states: 'And he gave unto Moses, when he had made an end of communing with him upon Mount Sinai, two tables of testimony, tables of stone, written with the finger of God.' God's finger would have to be like a chisel if we took this literally. Exodus 33:22 further states: 'And it shall come to pass, while my glory passeth by, that I will put thee in a cleft of the rock, and will cover thee with my hand while I pass by.' God would need a very big hand in order to cover Moses with it, wouldn't he?" When the Mormons hear these verses they will probably laugh and say, "Obviously they cannot be taken literally." "Then shouldn't the same principle apply to the verses you use, those that refer to parts of the body!"

Here is one more step that can be taken. Using the Mormon

172 · Approaching Mormons In Love

argument, you can prove that Satan also has a literal body. But Mormons believe that Satan is not permitted to have a body. They teach that Satan was denied a body because of the curse put upon him when he rebelled against God's plan of salvation. I ask Mormons, "Do you believe that Satan has a body?" They will usually answer "No." Then I explain that according to LDS logic Satan has to have a body.

Consider the following verses in light of the Mormon argument about bodies: Job 1:7: "And the Lord said unto Satan, Whence cometh thou? Then Satan answered the Lord, and said, From going to and fro in the earth, and from walking up and down in it." Don't the three bodily functions mentioned here imply that Satan has to have ears to hear, a mouth to speak, and legs to walk?

Revelation 20:1–2 states: "And I saw an angel come down from heaven, having the key of the bottomless pit and a great chain in his hand. And he laid hold of the dragon, that old serpent, which is the Devil and Satan, and bound him a thousand years." Doesn't Satan need a body in order to be bound with a chain? How can you bind a spirit with a chain?

Is Every Word Meant to Be Taken Literally?

Matthew 5:8—"Blessed are the pure in heart: for they shall see God." The Mormons also use this verse to try to prove that God can be seen. However, they disregard those scriptures that tell us that God is a spirit, invisible, and those that say that no man can see God and live. (See Exodus 33:20; Colossians 1:15; 1 Timothy 6:16; and 1 John 4:12.)

Ask the Mormon missionaries if they take all of Matthew 5 literally. Point out that verse 18 promises that none of the Bible will pass away. Yet Mormons believe that much of the Bible *has* been taken away. Then ask: "Do you believe that verse 13 talks about literal salt, and that verse 14 talks about literal light? Do you believe that the 'hell' mentioned in verses 22, 29, & 30 is literal? Also call their attention to verse 34: "Swear not at all; neither by heaven, for it is God's throne. . . ." The word "swear" here means to take a vow. Point out that Mormons don't obey this verse, because they take temple vows and various other oaths.

"The word 'shall' in verse 8 is in the future tense. If this verse promises literal sight of God in this life, how does the LDS Church explain Exodus 33:20 which says, 'And he [God] said, Thou canst not see my face; for there shall no man see me and live'? According to this verse, if Joseph Smith had seen God, he would have died immediately." (They might tell you that God cannot be seen under normal circumstances, but only if one is "quickened by the Spirit." If a man is not quickened, *then* he will die if he sees God.) The clincher here is that the Mormons teach that a person is not quickened until he is baptized! Joseph Smith had not been baptized at the time that he is supposed to have seen God!

Quite obviously, "shall" has to refer to the future, when we are in heaven and have been glorified.

Did Job Preexist?

Job 38:7—". . . when the morning stars sang together, and all the sons of God shouted for joy?" Mormons believe the use of the phrase "the sons of God" in this verse is proof that man exists in the "spirit world" before his physical birth on the earth. They say that because God asked (verse 4), "Where wast thou . . . ?", Job had to be somewhere—and it could only have been in this preexistent world. However, asking where Job was at that time does not mean that he had to exist somewhere. When the verse is read in context, it is obvious that Job was *not* there. In verse 28, God asks, "Hath the rain a father?" The answer, of course, is "No." In verse 29, He asks, "Out of whose womb came the ice?" We see from these examples that *poetic language* is being used repeatedly in this chapter.

Did Jeremiah Preexist?

Jeremiah 1:5—"Before I formed thee in the belly I knew thee; and before thou camest forth out of the womb I sanctified thee, and I ordained thee a prophet unto the nations." Mormons try to establish their doctrine of preexistent souls using the expression, "I knew thee." This verse only points out the fact that God has all knowledge. God thought about each one of us even before there was a world.

Does Lifelong Suffering Prove Preexistence?

John 9:2—"And his disciples asked him, saying, Master, who did sin, this man, or his parents, that he was born blind?" Mormons use this verse in their attempt to prove that man not only has a preexistence but that his actions in the preexistent world somehow determine his status in this world.

The Bible does not teach the preexistence of man. What the disciples were concerned about was the problem of suffering: Why are some people born into riches and some into poverty? Why are some people born healthy and some born sickly? The disciples were philosophizing instead of waiting to see what Christ would do for the blind man. The question they asked was not intended to imply a preexistence of the souls of men but was in line with the thinking of some of the Jews of that day. There were two main theories: (1) Some Jewish teachers taught that all lifelong suffering was to be attributed to the sins of one's parents. They derived this idea from Exodus 20:5: "Thou shalt not bow down thyself to them, nor serve them; for I the Lord thy God am a jealous God, visiting the iniquity of the fathers upon the children unto the third and forth generation of them that hate me." (2) Other Jewish teachers, however, held that a child could sin while still in the womb, citing Genesis 25:22: "And the children struggled together within her; and she said, If it be so, why am I thus? And she went to inquire of the Lord."

Jesus made it clear that both these theories are false. Rather, the purpose of *this* man's blindness was "that the works of God should be made manifest in him" (v. 3). His affliction was for the glory of God.

Does Baptism Regenerate a Person?

John 3:5—"Jesus answered, Verily, verily, I say unto thee, Except a man be born of water and of the Spirit, he cannot enter into the kingdom of God." Many groups, including the Mormons, use this verse to try to prove the doctrine of baptismal regeneration.

If baptism is essential to salvation, why did Christ himself never baptize anyone? (See John 4:2.) He came to "save his people from their sins." If baptism is essential to salvation, why did the Apostle Paul say, "Believe on the Lord Jesus Christ, and thou shalt be saved," when asked by the Philippian jailer what he must do to be saved (Acts 16:31)? If baptism is essential to salvation, why did Paul write the Corinthians saying, "I thank God that I baptized none of you, but Crispus and Gaius. . . . For Christ sent me not to baptize but to preach the gospel; not with wisdom of words, lest the cross of Christ should be made of none effect" (1 Corinthians 1:14, 17)? These verses make it clear that baptism is not essential to salvation nor is it a part of the gospel. (Some Mormons might equivocate and contend that Paul's practice was to lead converts to the place of baptism and then let one of his helpers baptize them. However, this is not the practice of Mormons.)

This passage in John must not be isolated but should be taken in the light of all scriptures. Notice how Jesus used the word "water" in other places in the Gospel of John. John 4:14: "But whosoever drinketh of the water that I shall give him shall never thirst; but the water that I shall give him shall be in him a well of water springing up into everlasting life." Water cannot mean baptism in that verse. John 7:37–38: "In the last day, that great day of the feast, Jesus stood and cried out, saying, If any man thirst, let him come unto me, and drink. He that believeth on me, as the scripture hath said, out of his heart shall flow rivers of living water." Here, again, the word "water" cannot mean baptism.

The word "water" in John 3:5 refers figuratively to the Word of God. There are a number of other figures of speech that likewise refer to God's Word. For instance, "Thy word is a lamp unto my feet, and a light unto my path" (Psalm 119:105). "Is not my word like as a fire, saith the Lord; and like a hammer that breaketh the rock in pieces?" (Jeremiah 23:29).

The following verses link the word "water" and the "Word of God" together. "Wherewithal shall a young man cleanse his way? By taking heed thereto according to thy word" (Psalm 119:9). "Now ye are clean through the word which I have spoken unto you" (John 15:3). "That he might sanctify and cleanse it with the washing of water by the word" (Ephesians 5:26).

Additional verses show the power that the Word of God has to change a life. "This is my comfort in my affliction: for thy word hath given me life" (Psalm 119:50). (Is not this what John 3:5 is saying? We are born again by the life-giving power of the Word of God.) "Of his own will begat he us with the word of truth, that we should be a kind of firstfruits of his creatures" (James 1:18). "Being born again, not of corruptible seed, but of incorruptible, by the word of God, which liveth and abideth for ever" (1 Peter 1:23). As the Word of God is preached, the Holy Spirit takes the Word and applies it to a person's heart. The Word shows us that we are sinners before God, but that Jesus Christ, as very God, died on the cross for our sins. As we confess our sins to God and appeal to Jesus Christ as our only Savior, we have new life and become children of God.

Note once again what John 3:5 *is* saying: "Except a man be born of water and of the Spirit, he cannot enter into the kingdom of God." Mormons do not believe what this verse says, that through the new birth we can enter into the kingdom of God—which is heaven. According to the Mormon definition, this would be the celestial kingdom. However, according to Mormon doctrine, one is not prepared for the celestial kingdom by just being baptized. The LDS Church teaches that repentance, faith, baptism and the receiving of the Holy Ghost are the basic requirements for membership into the Mormon church, and that through the Mormon church one might *work* toward the goal of exaltation. However, Mormon authorities admit that less than half of the members of the Mormon church will make it into the kingdom of God. Using just one word ("water") from this verse and ignoring the rest, as the Mormons do, is a blatant misuse of Scripture.

Mormons need to be shown what the new birth is. Nicodemus had physical life but he did not have spiritual life. All men need spiritual life—which is what "born again" means. It is receiving eternal life and a new heart, which Jesus Christ came to give. The new birth is not the reformation of the *outward* man; it is not the education of the *natural* man; it is not the purification of the *old* man; but it is the creation of a *new* man.

Are There Present-day Apostles and Prophets?

Ephesians 4:11—"And he gave some, apostles; and some, prophets; and some, evangelists; and some, pastors and teachers." Mormons quote this verse to try to prove that their church is the only true church because they have all of these, and especially apostles and prophets. However, it should be shown that they fail to fulfill this verse in a number of ways.

Mormons say that they have "evangelists," "pastors," and "teachers," but they use different names for them. Why don't they use the names given in the Bible? If they believe it is proper to use different names for these offices, why do they get upset when Christian churches do not mention the office of "apostle"? Mormon writings agree with us that the primary meaning of "apostle" is "sent one" or "missionary." Therefore, every missionary of the cross of Christ is an apostle in that sense. The true church *does* have apostles, but they are called by another name.

According to Mormonism, the only person who can become the president of the LDS Church (and thus a prophet) is someone who has been a member of the twelve apostles of their church. There are no Biblical grounds for such a requirement. If you ask a Mormon where the Bible teaches that a person must first be an apostle before he can be a prophet, he probably won't have an answer.

Are Prophets Essential Today?

Amos 3:7—"Surely the Lord God will do nothing, but he revealeth his secret unto his servants the prophets." Mormons quote this verse to try to prove the need for living prophets today. They say that everything God is going to do he reveals beforehand to his prophets. They insist that we need prophets today in order for God to rightly direct his people.

Hebrews 1:1–2 shows that in the past God spoke through prophets *but* in the *last days* (since Christ's ascension) God has spoken through his Son. Christ has been exalted and is now the Head of the Church. God has given all the revelation that we need: it is found in the Bible. Guidance is available to every Christian because Jesus has delivered his Word through the apostles once for all!

Is There a Present-day Aaronic Priesthood?

Hebrews 5:4—"And no man taketh this honor unto himself, but he that is called of God, as was Aaron." In the Mormon church, ordination is very important. This verse is used to try to prove the necessity of continuing the Old Testament priesthood in this present age (which the LDS Church calls the "Aaronic priesthood"). They make the following statement: "One must be ordained to the necessary priesthood by one having authority before he can administer the ordinances of the Gospel. Thus the Aaronic priesthood holds the keys of: a. The ministering of angels; b. The gospel of repentance; c. Baptism by immersion for the remission of sin" (From *A Marvelous Work And A Wonder*, by LeGrand Richards, page 84). The only problem is, there never was an "Aaronic priesthood." It was the "Levitical priesthood" which Aaron and his descendants ministered under, as successive "high priests."

However, it is claimed by Joseph Smith (*Doctrine and Covenants*, Section 13), that on May 15, 1829, an angel, acting under the direction of Peter, James and John, appeared to him and Oliver Cowdery and ordained them to the "Aaronic Priesthood." Joseph Smith declared that this gave him the necessary authority to organize the LDS Church and the kingdom of God upon the earth in this dispensation. Mormons therefore hold that Joseph Smith had the power to ordain others to the Aaronic priesthood, and so on down the line. And they use Hebrews 5:4 to argue that other churches are flawed because they do not have an Aaronic priesthood. So ask the Mormon you are dealing with to show you in the Bible where the very term "Aaronic priesthood" is mentioned by these two words. Of course, they cannot.

Putting the fact aside that there is no "Aaronic priesthood," there is another way you can show that the LDS Church is not based on the Bible. Aaron's ordination, under the Levitical priesthood, is described in great detail in Exodus 28, 29, 39, Leviticus 8–16 and Numbers 3:10. Mormons should be challenged about the way that they ordain people to the priesthood. They do not do it in the way that these passages require. Exodus 29:9, 29, 44,

Leviticus 8:36, and Numbers 3:10 clearly state that the priesthood is limited to those who are sons of Aaron—his direct descendants. Despite this, nearly all Mormon men hold the priesthood—yet few can prove that they are actual sons of Aaron. Sometimes Mormons will claim that when a person becomes a Mormon, his "Gentile" blood is exchanged for "Jewish" blood. They had to make up some sort of explanation to get around the fact that they are not true sons of Aaron and hence have no legitimate claim to being "priests" under the Levitical priesthood.

The Bible teaches that the need for a Levitical priesthood was done away with by the sacrifice of Jesus Christ on the cross. The main purpose of the O.T. priesthood was to provide a priest to act as mediator between God and the people. Now, with Christ as our mediator, we have free access to God through Jesus' blood and do not need a priest to take that office. Hebrews 7:12 states that the Levitical priesthood has been done away with because it has been fulfilled by Christ.

Don't False Prophecies Prove a Prophet False?

Matthew 7:21—"Not everyone that saith unto me, Lord, Lord, shall enter into the kingdom of heaven, but he that doeth the will of my Father which is in heaven." Mormons love to quote this verse to born-again people who have the assurance of eternal salvation. The believer ought to reply, "I am very glad that you brought this verse up. In the context of Matthew 7:13–23, this verse is speaking about the test of a prophet (see verse 22). It is the LDS Church which claims to have an earthly prophet, not Christians."

Mormons come under the scrutiny of this passage since they claim that Joseph Smith and the presidents of the church have all been prophets. Ask your visitors what sources they have outside of Mormon publications that can verify the truthfulness of Joseph Smith and the other prophets. They will claim that they have an "inward witness" as to the truth of Joseph Smith and do not need to investigate. However, this passage says nothing about an "inward witness." Jesus challenges all his followers to do "the will of my Father."

According to verse 22, some of those who call Jesus "Lord, Lord" will claim to have had the gift of prophecy. Joseph Smith claimed to have this gift, so the warning given here applies to him. What then should be our conclusion concerning the prophecies of Joseph Smith that were never fulfilled? Deuteronomy 18:20–22 gives both a warning and a clear test of a prophet: "But the prophet which shall presume to speak a word in my name which I have not commanded him to speak, or which shall speak in the name of other gods, even that prophet shall die. And if thou say in thine heart, How shall we know the word which the Lord hath not spoken? When a prophet speaketh in the name of the Lord, if the thing follow not, nor come to pass, that is the thing which the Lord hath not spoken, but the prophet hath spoken it presumptuously; thou shall not be afraid of him."

In short, all of a true prophet's prophecies will be fulfilled. How do the Mormons explain the following unfulfilled prophecies (See *Doctrine and Covenants* 84:1–5, 31, pages 153–54, and 155–56)? Here is a purported revelation given to Joseph Smith the Prophet at Kirtland, Ohio, on September 22 and 23, 1832:

> A revelation of Jesus Christ unto his servant Joseph Smith, Jun., and six elders, as they united their hearts and lifted their voices on high. Yea, the word of the Lord concerning his church, established in the last days for the restoration of his people, as he has spoken by the mouth of his prophets, and for the gathering of his saints to stand upon Mount Zion, which shall be the city of New Jerusalem. Which city shall be built, beginning at the temple lot, which is appointed by the finger of the Lord, in the western boundaries of the State of Missouri and dedicated by the hand of Joseph Smith, Jun., and others with whom the Lord was well

pleased. Verily this is the word of the Lord, that the city New Jerusalem shall be built by the gathering of the saints, beginning at this place, even the place of the temple, which temple shall be reared in this generation. For verily this generation shall not all pass away until an house shall be built unto the Lord, and a cloud shall rest upon it, which cloud shall be even the glory of the Lord, which shall fill the houses . . . which house shall be built unto the Lord in this generation, upon the consecrated spot as I have appointed.

This prophecy declares that a Mormon temple shall be built on a specified piece of land in Independence, Missouri, and that it would be built within the lifetime of those who heard Joseph Smith give the prophecy. To this day the temple has *not* been built, and this lot is owned by the Reorganized Church of Jesus Christ of Latter-day Saints (now called the Community of Christ)—and they are in no mood to sell it to the LDS Church of Salt Lake City because there is no friendly relationship between the two. Also, I do not know of anyone living today who heard Joseph Smith give this prophecy in 1832.

It is obvious that this prophecy has not been fulfilled! It referred to the generation that was living at that time (1832). On the basis of this unfulfilled prophecy, Joseph Smith must be classified as a *false prophet*.

Some Mormons will say that this prophecy did not refer to the generation living at that time. However, Mormon writers clearly interpret the prophecy as meaning the generation living when the prophecy was given. Quotations from three of these writers are given below:

And let me remind you that it is predicted that this generation shall not pass away till a temple shall be built, and the glory of the Lord rest upon it, according to the promise (Geo. A. Smith, *Journal of Discourses*, Vol. 9, p. 71, March 10, 1861).

The day is near when a temple shall be reared in the Center Stake of Zion, and the Lord has said His glory shall rest on that House in this generation, that is the generation in which the revelation was given, which is upwards of thirty years ago (Geo. Q. Cannon, *Journal of Discourses*, Vol. 10, p. 344, Oct. 23, 1864).

God has been with us from the time that we came to this land, and I hope that the day of our tribulations are past. I hope this, because God promised in the year 1832 that we should, before the generation then living had passed away, return and build up the City of Zion in Jackson County; that we should return and build up the temple of the Most High where we formerly laid the corner stone. He promised us that He would manifest Himself on that temple, and that the glory of God should be upon it; and not only upon the temple, but within it, even a cloud by day and a flaming fire by night.

The Latter-day Saints just as much expect to receive a fulfillment of that promise during the generation that was in existence in 1832 as they expect that the sun will rise and set tomorrow. Why? Because God can't lie. He will fulfill all His promises. He has spoken; it must come to pass. This is our faith (Orson Pratt, *Journal of Discourses*, Vol. 13, p. 362, May 5, 1870).

There are yet other statements by Mormon writers on the subject, but these are adequate to show that "this generation" meant those living at the time Joseph Smith gave the prophecy in 1832. A temple has not been built in Jackson County, Missouri. Another unfulfilled prophecy reads like this:

The Mayor, Alderman, and Cancelers signed officially the Memorial to Congress for redress of losses and grievances in Missouri. While discussing the petition to Congress, I prophesied, by virtue of the holy Priesthood vested in me, and in the name of the Lord Jesus Christ, that, if Congress will not hear our petition and grant us protection, they shall be broken up as a government . . . and there shall nothing be left of them—not even a grease spot

(Joseph Smith, *History of the Church*, Vol. 6, p. 116, Dec. 1843. Also *Millennial Star*, Vol. 22, p. 455).

The Congress of the United States of America did not make redress for the losses, and the American government has not been "broken up as a government." This, then, is another false prophecy by Joseph Smith.

Joseph Smith's teaching about the "inhabitants on the moon" is either ignored or denied by Mormons today. Too embarrassing to be repudiated, it is usually swept under the rug. The Prophet declared:

> The inhabitants on the moon are more of a uniform size than the inhabitants of the earth, being about 6 foot in height. They dress very much like the Quaker style and are quite uniform in style, or the fashion of the dress. They live to be very old; coming generally, near a thousand years (*Journal of Oliver B. Huntington*, Vol. 3, p. 166 of typed copy at Utah State Historical Society).

This vivid description of these moon men was given by Joseph the seer, and he supposedly could "see" whatever he asked the Father in the name of Jesus to see!

For many years after Joseph Smith's death, Mormons continued to teach that the moon was inhabited. As late as 1892, the concept that the moon was inhabited appeared in a Church publication, *The Young Woman's Journal*, Vol. 3, pp. 263–64, 1892. The following quote is taken directly from this publication:

THE INHABITANTS ON THE MOON
by O.B. Huntington

Astronomers and philosophers have, from time almost immemorial until very recently, asserted that the moon was uninhabited, that it had no atmosphere, etc. But recent discoveries, through the means of powerful telescopes, have given scientists a doubt or two upon the old theory. Nearly all the great discoveries of men in the last half century have, in one way or another, either directly or indirectly, contributed to prove Joseph Smith to be a Prophet.

As far back as 1837, I know that he said the moon was inhabited by men and women the same as this earth, and that they lived to a greater age than we do—that they live generally to near the age of 1000 years. He described the men as averaging near six feet in height, and dressing quite uniformly in something near the Quaker style.

In my Patriarchal blessing, given by the father of Joseph the Prophet in Kirtland, 1837, I was told that I should preach the gospel before I was 21 years of age; that I should preach the gospel to the inhabitants upon the islands of the sea, and—to the inhabitants on the moon, even the planet you can now behold with your eyes.

The first two promises have been fulfilled, and the later may be verified. For the verification of two promises we may reasonably expect the third to be fulfilled also.

It is common knowledge that people do not live on the moon, despite the striking statement by Joseph Smith. Yes, Joseph Smith gave prophesies, but they were false prophecies, thus showing that Joseph Smith will not enter into the kingdom of heaven.

Is the Image of God in Man a Physical Likeness?

Genesis 1:26–27; 5:1–3—"And God said, Let us make man in our image, after our likeness: and let them have dominion over the fish of the sea, and over the fowl of the air, and over the cattle, and over all the earth, and over every creeping thing that creepeth upon the earth. So God created man in his own image, in the image of God created he him; male and female created he them." These verses are used by the Mormons to try to prove that God has a body. They reason that if we are made in the likeness of God then God must be like us and have a body. They also use Genesis 5:1–3 which says: "This is the book of the generations of Adam. In the day that God created man, in the likeness of God made he him; male and female created he them: and blessed them, and called their name Adam, in the day when they were created. And Adam lived an hundred and thirty years, and begat a son in his likeness, after his image; and called his name Seth." Mormons say that since Seth was in the bodily likeness of his father Adam, and Adam was created in the likeness of God, consequently God had to have a body.

In Genesis 1:26–27, the "image and likeness" of God is found chiefly in the fact that man is a personal, rational, and moral being. While God is infinite and man is finite, nevertheless man possesses the elements of personality similar to those of the divine Person: thinking (Genesis 2:19–20), feeling (Genesis 3:6), and will (Genesis 3:6–7). The Bible never says that God has a body like man. It talks about the various body parts (hands, ears, eyes, etc.) of God but these are not to be taken in the literal sense. The Bible clearly teaches that God is a *Spirit*: "God is a Spirit; and they that worship him must worship him in spirit and in truth" (John 4:24). The resurrected Christ, who did have a body, said in Luke 24:39, "Behold my hands and my feet, that it is I myself: handle me, and see; for a spirit hath not flesh and bones, as ye see me have."

Mormons claim that *The Book of Mormon* contains the fullness of the gospel. *The Book of Mormon* nowhere says that God has a body and is approximately six-feet tall like men living today. However, *The Book of Mormon* does teach that God is "a spirit." Alma 18:24–28 says: "And Ammon began to speak unto him with boldness, and said unto him: Believest thou that there is a God? And he answered, and said unto him: I do not know what that meaneth. And then Ammon said: Believest thou that there is a Great Spirit? And he said, Yea. And Ammon said: This is God. And Ammon said unto him again: Believest thou that this Great Spirit, who is God, created all things which are in heaven and in the earth?" This passage clearly teaches that the creator God is "Spirit."

Likewise, Alma 19:25–27 says: "And it came to pass that there were many among them who said that Ammon was the Great Spirit, and others said he was sent by the Great Spirit; but others rebuked them all, saying that he was a monster, who had been sent from the Nephites to torment them. And there were some who said that Ammon was sent by the Great Spirit to afflict them because of their iniquities; and that it was the Great Spirit that had always attended the Nephites, who had ever delivered them out of their hands; and they said that it was this Great Spirit who had destroyed so many of their brethren, the Lamanites."

And again, in Alma 22:9–11: "And the king said: Is God that Great Spirit that brought our fathers out of the land of Jerusalem? And Aaron said unto him: Yea, he is that Great Spirit, and he created all things both in heaven and in earth. Believest thou this? And he said: Yea, I believe that the Great Spirit created all things, and I desire that ye should tell me concerning all these things, and I will believe thy words."

It is strange that the Mormons believe God has a body when both the Bible and *The Book of Mormon* state conclusively that God is a "Spirit."

Another important point about the Genesis 1:26–27 passage is the use of the plural "us," "our image," and "our likeness." Mormons teach that only God had a body at the time of creation (or the gathering together of matter). They have trouble explaining why the plurals are used if these phrases refer to a single body.

How Is Christ the Image of God?

Hebrews 1:3—"Who, being the brightness of his glory, and the express image of his person, and upholding all things by the word of his power, when he had by himself purged our sins, sat down on the right hand of the Majesty of high." Mormons try to show that since Christ, who had a body, was the "image" of God, then God surely has to have a body. That interpretation is refuted in Colossians 1:15, which speaks of Christ as "the image of the invisible God, the firstborn of every creature." It clearly states that God is "invisible." This "invisible" image is not that of a body.

One further point: A Mormon should not be allowed to use Hebrews 1:3 without being confronted with the need to be "purged" of sin. This verse can be used evangelistically, for it shows that salvation is rooted in the finished work of God's Son who now reigns on high.

What Constitutes the Foundation of the Church?

Ephesians 2:20; 4:5—In Ephesians 2:20, Christians are said to be "built upon the foundation of the apostles and prophets, Jesus Christ himself being the chief corner stone." Mormons argue that this verse shows the need for apostles and prophets in the church today. However, this verse is talking about the "foundation" and not the building (God's household). The apostles and prophets laid the foundation of the church. The writings and teachings of the apostles and prophets have been recorded so that we know how the church is to be structured. All true born-again Christians are built upon the same foundation. That foundation is the gospel of Christ, as witnessed to by the apostles and prophets. That foundation has been laid once-for-all upon the authority of Christ. It is found in the Bible.

The Mormon church, on the other hand, is still in the stage of laying a foundation. Many of the teachings of the Mormon church have changed and are continuing to change, because they do not have a sure foundation for their church.

Ephesians 4:5 says there is "One Lord, one faith, one baptism." Mormons claim that the LDS Church is the "one faith" and that all other churches are corrupt. Yet there are 83 different church groups which point to Joseph Smith as their founder. Each group charges that the other groups are improperly structured or apostate.

The Mormons say that the existence of many different Christian denominations proves that there is not one faith among Christians but many *conflicting* faiths. However, in spite of denominational differences, all true Bible-believing Christians agree about six major doctrines:

(1) The Bible is the Word of God and its message is free of error; (2) Jesus Christ was born of a virgin; (3) Jesus is truly God and truly man; (4) Christ died as the perfect sacrifice for all our sins; (5) Jesus rose bodily from the grave and ascended into heaven; and (6) the Lord Jesus Christ is coming back again in great glory. These doctrines are the nucleus of the gospel and are exactly what the Mormon needs to hear.

Is Salvation Based on Human Works?

Philippians 2:12—"Wherefore, my beloved, as ye have always obeyed, not as in my presence only, but now much more in my absence, work out your own salvation with fear and trembling." Mormons use this verse to teach that a person is saved on the basis of his own works. However, they should be shown that works cannot earn salvation (Romans 4:5; Titus 3:5–7). The work of God is to have faith in Christ. Jesus said: "This is the work of God, that ye believe on him whom he [the Father] hath sent" (John 6:29). Christ alone is the basis for our salvation. Only those who believe on Him as Savior and Lord are doing the work of God.

Is Baptism Necessary for Salvation?

Acts 2:38—"Then Peter said unto them, Repent, and be baptized every one of you in the name of Jesus Christ for the remission of sins, and ye shall receive the gift of the Holy Ghost." Mormons claim this verse proves that baptism is necessary for salvation. They mean that baptism is necessary to get into the Mormon church so that they can work for their salvation. But the verse says that the remission of sins comes through the Lord Jesus Christ. It does not say anything about becoming a member of a certain church.

Furthermore, Acts 10:47–48 indicates that salvation does not come through water baptism: "Can any man forbid water, that these should not be baptized, which have received the Holy Ghost as well as we? And he commanded them to be baptized in the name of the Lord." In these verses, belief came before baptism. In Acts 11:17, where Peter is commenting on this passage, quoted above, he says, "Forasmuch then as God gave them the like gift as he did unto us, who believed on the Lord Jesus Christ; what was I, that I could withstand God?" Peter says that they believed and received the Holy Spirit, and then were baptized. Mormons don't practice this order of events, because they believe that baptism comes first, followed by the coming of the Holy Spirit through the laying on of hands by someone in authority. Though they claim to have the "restored gospel," it is plain that their practice is different from that found in the Bible. Baptism is not necessary to salvation, but is a sign showing that someone has died in Jesus Christ and has risen with new life in Him.

Was There a Falling Away of the True Church?

2 Thessalonians 2:3—"Let no man deceive you by any means: for that day shall not come, except there come a falling away first, and that man of sin be revealed, the son of perdition." The Mormons use this verse as evidence that there was a "falling away" and that the church was restored by Joseph Smith. They believe this falling away happened around A.D. 400. But in the vast amount of material on the early church that is available to re-

searchers there is no description of the early church that is similar to today's Mormon church. Consequently, it is evident that Joseph Smith did not restore the true church, because a restoration needs to be exactly like the original.

Moreover, there has never been a complete falling away. Jesus said in Matthew 16:18: "And I say also unto thee, That thou art Peter, and upon this rock I will build my church: and the gates of hell shall not prevail against it." Though toil and strife, attacks from within and without, God has guided His church through twenty centuries. She has been rent apart by schisms. She has suffered from character faults. Yet she has kept the faith to which all Christians have at all times subscribed. And that faith has been expressed in the great historic creeds of Christendom. If there was a complete falling away, then the gates of hell *did* prevail: but we know that no promise of Jesus has ever failed, so there has never been a complete falling away.

In the *Doctrine and Covenants*, Section 7, it says that John, the beloved disciple, never died. According to Mormon writings, one true apostle is still living today, so there could have not been a complete falling away. If the Apostle John is still living, as Joseph Smith claimed, why didn't God use him instead of giving completely new revelations to Joseph Smith?

Is Prayer the Way to Test a Religion?

James 1:5—"If any of you lack wisdom, let him ask of God, that giveth to all men liberally, and upbraideth not, and it shall be given him." Mormons use this verse to support their view that you can ascertain whether a religion is true or not simply by praying about it. It has become their favorite tool. They know if you investigate Scripture, you will never join the LDS Church. Some of the many verses which deal with testing prophets and religions are : 1 John 4:1–3; Matthew 7:15; 1 Thessalonians 5:21; 1 Timothy 4:1–2; 1 Timothy 4:3–4; 1 Peter 2:1–19; Jude 4, 16; Revelation 2:2; Deuteronomy 13; and Jeremiah 23:9–40. The way to identify a true religion is not simply by praying, but by testing its claims according to the clear teachings of God's Word.

Chapter Fourteen

Thought-Provoking Questions

$\mathbf{A}$S I said before, when dealing with Mormons you have to get them involved with material and questions they are not familiar with in order to make them think. Here are some questions I have found helpful. As you converse, go through these matters very slowly. You will not receive any reasonable answers to these questions because *there are none*, but these queries are for the specific purpose of making them *think*— which is necessary if they are to leave the Mormon church. (Once you learn what kinds of questions to ask to provoke them to think, you can then devise your own questions.)

1. The LDS Church teaches that it is *absolutely necessary* to have a physical body in order to start a person on the road to becoming "a god." In bold contradiction to this belief, it teaches also that Jesus was the Jehovah-God of the Old Testament.

Question. How could Jesus be the Jehovah-God of the Old Testament when he was still in a spirit form and had not yet received an earthly body? He hadn't even begun the process of becoming a god, let alone being the Mighty God who is revealed in the Bible. Please enlighten me.

· · ·

2. The Mormons will talk about the Holy Ghost, but if you

194 · Approaching Mormons In Love

ask them how he came to be as he is, they will not be able to give any answer. LDS doctrine, however, maintains that he is a member of the Godhead, having great power and authority.

Question. Since the Holy Ghost is recognized to be God, and yet is "a spirit" and does not have a physical body, then how could he be "God"? Don't you teach that becoming "a god" is a process, and that a physical body is necessary for this? Furthermore, I've never read that the Holy Ghost will receive a body in the future; consequently he will never be able to have a world of his own like the Father. And doesn't your church teach that the curse on Satan was that he would "never receive a body"? Yet the Holy Ghost, who is perfectly holy, seems to be cursed like Satan! Could you please explain this to me?

. . .

3. Mormons talk a lot about the ministry of angels, whom they recognize as spirit beings.

Question. The Bible has much to say about angels, and many times they are classified as "holy" angels. So it would seem that in the preexistent world—according to Mormon doctrine—they were the *best* spirit beings. Your church teaches (or at least it once taught) that the *more valiant* a spirit was in the preexistent state, the *better* its lot will be in *this* world. Right? But we find that at the end of this world there are *still* angels who have never received a body so they can work at becoming a god. For example, there are a number of Bible verses which state that the holy angels will be the reapers at the end of the age. (See Matthew 13:39, 41; 24:31; 25:31.) It seems that being a holy angel is quite a disadvantage! Could you explain to me why these holy angels will never receive a human body? (They might speculate, but don't accept their answer. Ask them to show you in Mormon literature where their answer is found. Of course, this cannot be done.)

. . .

4. Mormons teach that Abraham has already been exalted—

has become a god and governs his own world. Strangely, how-ever, they do not believe that Jesus Christ has become a god and governs *his* own world. Rather, they claim that Christ has charge of the terrestrial kingdom (which is a lesser kingdom than the celestial kingdom). If this is true, then obviously he does not have his own world, according to their teaching.

Question. It seems to me that if Christ had a head start above all who have lived on this earth, that he would be the first one to become a god! (After all, they teach he was God in Old Testa-ment times.) Could you explain to me why imperfect Abraham has already become a god, but Jesus Christ, who was the most righteous person who ever lived, has not become a god and re-ceived his own world?

• • •

5. Mormons teach that each human has already lived in two places as a spirit: (1) in intelligence, (2) in the spirit world, before his spirit came to this world and received a body to dwell in. They maintain that the memory of these two existences has been entirely forgotten.

Question. I understand that the LDS Church teaches that a person's memory of his or her two previous existences as a spirit, before coming to this earth, is wiped away when one is born onto the planet. I have two questions concerning this.

1. It is evident from the Bible that when people leave this world and go into the next, they do not lose the memory of their earthly existence. In Luke 16:25—I'm sure you know the story about the rich man and Lazarus—Abraham says to the rich man in hell, "Son, *remember* that in your lifetime you received your good things, and likewise Lazarus evil things. . . ." Surely Abraham would not tell the man to do what is *impossible*! Since the memory of this *earthly* existence is not wiped away, I cannot see that there is any advantage in forgetting everything one learned in the *pre-vious* world! (I don't believe this, but am just showing how their

teachings are not consistent.) It seems to me that the experiences met with over those many years would be very helpful on this earth. After all, we were then living with the Father! This surely was a wonderful time and worth remembering. Could you give me some logical reason why the memory of our previous existences is always wiped away?

2. The experience of Jesus is not consistent with this Mormon teaching. In John 17:2, 22, and 24 it is very clear that Jesus Christ remembered the existence that he had with the Father before he came to this earth, and it was a place of glory and splendor. Since your church teaches that Jesus was no different from any of the other spirits in the previous world, but just happened to be the first one born, then why did Jesus clearly *remember* and why do all the rest of the spirits *forget*?

• • •

6. The LDS Church teaches that Mormons can have their children sealed to them for "time and eternity" through a temple ceremony. (If the nuptials were performed in the temple, then the children are automatically sealed to them without an additional service.) This means that if they make it to the celestial kingdom they can all live together as a family. But Mormon doctrine also states that each male Mormon has the potential of becoming "a god," receiving *his own* world—and at this time he and his wife or wives will be able to start a whole new race of spirits. If this is true, and a father's sons can each become a god and each have his own world, then it would be impossible for them to live together as families.

Question. Since the Mormon church teaches that every male has the potential of becoming "a god" and receiving his own world, then how is it possible that families can live together for eternity, since a father's sons would all have the possibility of becoming "a god" and living on separate worlds. To me, this is an enigma! How do you solve this complicated problem?

· · · ·

7. Mormons believe that there are many "gods" and that it is possible for sinful man to work himself up to be "a god." In fact, their religion boils down to a complex system of good works for achieving godhood. So they constantly refer to James 2:20: "But wilt thou know, O vain man, that faith without works is dead?" However, the verse just before this—James 2:19—says, "Thou believest that there is one God; thou doest well. . . ." (Yes, they use one verse and disregard the other.) In John 17:3 we find: "And this is life eternal, that they might know thee the only true God, and Jesus Christ whom thou hast sent." Thus the Bible (and *The Book of Mormon* likewise, we have seen) clearly declares that there is only *one* God and that He is the *true* God.

Question. (You should have them read James 2:19 and John 17:3 before you ask the question.) How do you justify the teachings of the LDS Church that there are many gods when the Bible and *The Book of Mormon* teach that there is just one God and that He is the *true* God? Doesn't this make all other gods false gods?

(They will likely weasel out of this by declaring: "There are many gods, but only one with whom we have to do.")

Question #2. I understand that Mormons believe that the Father is God, that the Son is God, and that Holy Spirit is God—which makes three gods. (They do not believe in "the" Trinity, which is one God manifested in three persons. They believe in "a" trinity, which refers to the Father, Son, and Holy Spirit, but deny that they have been eternally God and that they are equal in power, knowledge, and essence. This is much different from the Christian view of the Trinity.) If you have to do with only "one" God, then which one are you referring to? Are you saying that you only have a connection with the Father and not with the Son and Holy Spirit? Or are you saying you have to do only with Jesus Christ (since this is in the name of your church), and not the Father or the Holy Spirit? Or are you saying you conduct business only with the Holy Spirit and not the Father or the Son? (This will be difficult for them to answer.)

• • •

8. As I stated before, Mormons believe in a long succession of gods. They will say, "What father didn't have a father!" To them, this settles the question—the process of becoming gods has been going on for many eons. They also teach that all of these gods are continuing to increase in status. This concept means that the gods above them are much more advanced, making each subsequent god inferior to some degree.

Question. There are quite a number of passages in the Bible that declare that the God of the Bible-believing Christian is "the most high God." (See Genesis 14:18, Numbers 24:16, Psalm 78:35, Daniel 4:25; 7:27, etc.) If there really are other "gods," surely this means that all these other gods, including the god whom you serve, are inferior to the God whom I believe in and serve. My God is perhaps a billion times greater than your god! Why are you satisfied with such an inferior god when you could become a child of the most high God through faith in Jesus Christ as your matchless, most high Redeemer?

• • •

9. The Mormons teach that God has a physical body. One of the ways they try to prove this is to show you places in the Bible where God is portrayed as having hands, arms, a back, plus the ability to speak (so he must have a mouth) and to see (so he must have eyes), etc.

Question. I understand that the Mormons believe that God has a physical body and your church tries to prove this by mentioning certain body parts that God is said to possess. If this is really true, then God also has to be a "bird," because the psalmist mentions that He has wings and feathers. (See Psalm 17:8; 36:7; 57:1; 63:7; and 91:4.)

They will likely reply that these are obviously just "figures of speech."

You should then ask them why we can't say the same thing regarding the parts of the human body that are mentioned in relation to God, since the Bible clearly affirms that God is "spirit."

· · · ·

10. Mormons teach that the curse put upon Satan for rebelling against the Father was that he could never receive a physical body, which bars him from the privilege of working towards "exaltation"—that is, becoming a god.

Question. Your church teaches that Lucifer—now known as Satan—was barred from exaltation by not being allowed to have a physical body. But doesn't the Bible speak about Satan having physical parts? In Job 1:7 the Lord "spoke" to Satan, so he surely has to have ears. Satan "answered" God, so he must have a mouth. This same verse speaks about Satan "walking up and down" in the earth; surely Satan has to have legs in order to walk. Why shouldn't these statements prove that Satan has a physical body?— because this is the very way the LDS Church tries to prove that *God* has a physical body!

· · · ·

11. Mormons will admit that Mormonism cannot be based solely on the Bible. But Mormonism is clearly not based upon *The Book of Mormon* either! In fact, what is taught in *The Book of Mormon* is largely the opposite of what the LDS Church teaches. In order to find out what the Mormons *really* believe, one has to read the other approved Mormon publications, like *Doctrine and Covenants*, *The Pearl of Great Price*, and the writings and recorded speeches of Joseph Smith and others who succeeded him.

Question. Since Mormon doctrine is not found in *The Book of Mormon,* then why isn't it reasonable to conclude that the people mentioned in *The Book of Mormon* could not be true Mormons— since they did not have the "modern-day revelations" which today's Mormons claim *they* have been given?

Conclusion

WHEN I speak about witnessing to Mormons, a common question I'm asked is: "How many Mormons have you seen delivered and saved?" This is because the average Christian has yet to meet anyone who has been converted from Mormonism; so it is not surprising for him to wonder if it's possible to win them to Christ. However, when one becomes involved in witnessing to Mormons, he or she hears of many who have been saved! It is possible to see Mormons leave the great bondage that they are in and *come into the glorious freedom of Christ!* I can attest to this. The sad part is that most Christians have left the witnessing to those who themselves have come out of Mormonism. I praise the Lord for these courageous people, but in order to have a greater impact on Mormonism more Christians need to become involved. I feel the spread of Mormonism can be *stopped*, but it will take many more Christians witnessing to do this.

One advantage we have is that the Mormons are coming right to our doors. If in your case they are not, you can respond to one of their ads and ask for the material they are offering—and you will shortly be visited by two missionaries. At first, your Mormon visitors will be very bold and will seem to be very confident, but all of this is on the surface. I have dealt with enough Mor-

202 · Approaching Mormons In Love

mons to know that they are woefully empty. Some Mormons are truly looking for something to satisfy the hunger of their souls. I know of one Mormon missionary who went to every church (about 32 of them) in the town where he was stationed to see if they had something better to offer than what he had. Of course, he did not state his real motive for visiting these churches, but that was his underlying incentive. (He told me this in a letter.) At not one of these 32 churches did he meet anyone who took the time or had the patience to get to know him so that they could present the true gospel to this young man.

I had a very interesting experience once. A Christian lady had opened her home and she and I were meeting regularly with two Mormon missionaries. At one session she casually remarked, "Didn't you Mormon missionaries until recent times ride bicycles? But now I see you are driving cars. Who owns the cars?"

"The Church purchases the cars and we missionaries pay to use them," one blurted out.

"And who buys the gas?"

"Oh, we have to buy the gas! Otherwise, some of our fellows would tear up the streets with them."

He read the astonishment on my face. "Get off of it!" he said. "You know why a lot of us are out on our missions. Some guys just want to get away from their parents—or from a girlfriend. They don't want to work for a couple of years; or they want a new adventure and to see new places!"

I responded, "I don't see how you can put much confidence in some of your fellow missionaries."

"I guess you can't," he frankly admitted.

Many Christians have written off Mormons as not being able to be saved without even *trying* to witness to them, but I know from personal experience they *can* be saved. With the information in this book and a lot of love and prayer, you can give a faithful witness to our wonderful Lord and Savior Jesus Christ. This is the longing and prayer of my heart.

Appendix 1

Similarities between Mormonism and Islam

1. Joseph Smith received revelations from angels.
2. He alone saw and "translated" the gold plates of Nephi.
3. The Book of Mormon claims to be "another testament to Christ."
4. In a vision, Joseph Smith was explicitly told by Jesus not to join any other churches because they were all false. Through him Christ "restored" the church.
5. Mormonism teaches salvation by human good works.
6. Mormonism teaches the perfectibility of human nature.
7. Mormonism permitted polygamy until the U.S, Government outlawed the practice. It maintains it in principle.
8. The Church of Jesus Christ of Latter-day Saints (LDS) is gathered around Salt Lake City, Utah, as its religious center.
9. Mormonism aggressively recruits members around the globe. Its early history saw the use of violence on its journey to Utah.

1. Muhammad received revelations from an angel.
2. The revelations were private and not open to scrutiny.
3. The Qur'an claims to be God's final revelation after the *Taurat* (Torah) and the *Injeel* (Gospel).
4. Islam claims to be the last and perfect completion of the monotheistic faiths. Islam supercedes Judaism and Christianity.
5. Islam teaches a salvation by human good works.
6. Islam teaches the perfectibility of human nature.
7. Islam permits polygamy.
8. Islam identifies itself with a greater international community gathered around Mecca as its religious center.
9. Islam is militantly expansionistic. Its history is marked by violence.

10. Mormonism experienced a leadership split between those who followed the family of Joseph Smith (Reorganized LDS) and those who followed Brigham Young as President of the Utah Church.

11. Mormonism went on to establish a largely social and business empire following the forced termination of its political entity.

12. Although international in scope, the LDS Church retains a very "White Anglo-Saxon Protestant" American pioneer cultural ethos in its style, dress, and demeanor. Strong emphasis on uniformity.

10. Islam experienced a leadership crisis around the issue of succession: family of Muhammad (Shi'a) versus the chosen leader, or Caliph, of the Muslim community (Sunni).

11. Islam went on to establish an empire, with successive empires ruling on the same basis as the original Muslim vision. Although fragmented today, Islam maintains a strong sense of Islamic unity around the Five Pillars and Mecca.

12. Although international in scope, Islam retains a strong Arabic identity in its religious language, its theology and practice. Strong emphasis on uniformity.

— *Source unknown.*

Appendix 2

Source Material on Mormonism

AT first it is very hard to get a Mormon to read any kind of "sectarian" literature, so that is why you need to witness to them as I have suggested in this book. But after you have met together a number of times and they realize that you are sincere and have a real burden for their soul, they may begin to question their own religion and then you will have a greater likelihood of getting them to read other material. One book I have found particularly helpful is *Mormonism, Shadow or Reality?* by Jerald and Sandra Tanner (former Mormons), which you can order from them. Their address is: Utah Lighthouse Ministry, Box 1884, Salt Lake City Utah 84110. I have been able to place over 100 copies of this book in the hands of Mormons. Once a Mormon reads this book he is almost sure to leave Mormonism, as I have seen. You will want to read it yourself and keep copies on hand so that you can get them into the hands of Mormons as you deal with them.

I also highly recommend: *A View of the Hebrews*, by Ethan Smith. This is truly an eyeopener. When a Mormon reads this book, he can easily see how Joseph Smith used it in writing *The Book of Mormon*. Another good book to have on hand is *The Bible and Mormon Doctrine*, by Sandra Tanner. These also are available from Utah Lighthouse Ministry.

If you have any questions or want documentation, please feel free to contact me at: 6-B Swift Lane, Whiting, NJ 08759-2922 or telephone me at (732)350-0735.

• DO YOU FEEL LIKE HIDING . . .
when Jehovah's Witnesses ring your doorbell? •

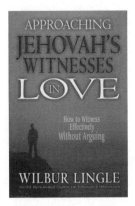

Trade Paper ISBN 0-87508-778-7

Have you tried to convey your faith to them . . . and gotten nowhere?

_____

THEN THIS BOOK IS FOR YOU!

_____

A proven and practical guide which includes questions, answers, conversation starters and other great witnessing tools!

This book was produced by CLC Publications. We hope it has been life-changing and has given you a fresh experience of God through the work of the Holy Spirit. CLC Publications is an outreach of CLC International, a global literature mission with work in over 50 countries. If you would like to know more about us or are interested in opportunities to serve with a faith mission, we invite you to contact us at:

CLC Ministries International
P.O. Box 1449
Fort Washington, PA 19034
—

Phone: (215) 542-1242
E-mail: clcmail@clcusa.org
www.clcusa.org

DO YOU LOVE GOOD CHRISTIAN BOOKS?
Do you have a heart for worldwide missions?

You can receive a FREE subscription to:
Floodtide,
(CLC's magazine on global literature missions).

Order by e-mail at:

floodtide@clcusa.org
or fill in the coupon below and mail to:

**P.O. Box 1449,
Fort Washington, PA 19034.**

FREE FLOODTIDE SUBSCRIPTION!

Name: _____

Address: _____

_____

Phone: _____ E-mail: _____

READ THE REMARKABLE STORY OF
the founding of
CLC INTERNATIONAL

"Any who doubt that Elijah's God still lives ought to read of the money supplied when needed, the stores and houses provided and the appearance of personnel in answer to prayer.

—Moody Monthly

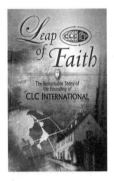

Is it possible that the printing press, the editor's desk, the Christian bookstore, and the mail order department, can glow with the fast-moving drama of an "Acts of the Apostles"?

Find out, as you are carried from two people in an upstairs bookroom to a worldwide chain of Christian bookcenters, multiplied by nothing but a "shoestring" of faith and committed, though sometimes unlikely, lives.